Materialien für den bilingualen Unterricht

Going CLIL

Prep Course

Heiner Böttger · Oliver Meyer

Inhalt

Scenario 1		From town to town	
		Orientation in a city	4
Scenario 2		Where I come from	
		Germany and beyond	12
Scenario 3		When in Rome …	
		Ancient Rome	20
Scenario 4		Off to Europe	
		Tourism	28
Scenario 5		Stormy weather ahead	
		Weather forecasts	36
Scenario 6		Of knights and ladies	
		The Middle Ages	46
Scenario 7		Paradise in danger	
		The rainforest	56
Scenario 8		The hobbits of Flores	
		Prehistoric Man	64
Scenario 9		Snow in motion	
		Avalanche!	74
Skills pages			84
Self-assessment pages			86
Quellenverzeichnis			88

Vorwort

Liebe Schülerinnen und Schüler,

Going CLIL – Prep Course soll Euch systematisch darauf vorbereiten, im bilingualen Sachfachunterricht Fächer wie Erdkunde, Geschichte oder Wirtschaft auf Englisch in den Griff zu bekommen. Dazu ist es beispielsweise ganz wichtig, mit Originaltexten oder Filmen umgehen zu können.

Wir zeigen Euch, wie ihr sie verstehen könnt, auch wenn ihr nicht jedes Wort kennt. Ihr lernt auch, Bilder systematisch zu beschreiben, damit es euch später keine Probleme macht, historische Abbildungen oder Satellitenbilder auszuwerten. Wir helfen euch, mit Tabellen und Statistiken umzugehen oder aus Stichpunkten einen Text zu konstruieren. Und wir wollen euer Gedächtnis trainieren. Deswegen enthalten alle Szenarien Texte zum Auswendiglernen.

In den Texten begegnen euch immer wieder die gleichen Symbole:

💡 Das Wort vor dem Zeichen habt ihr möglicherweise noch nicht gelernt, aber es ähnelt einem euch bekannten Wort in Deutsch oder Englisch. Bekommt ihr es heraus?

Words Hier werden schwierige Wörter erklärt, die ihr nicht kennt. Das heißt nicht, dass ihr sie lernen müsst, denn manchmal sind sie sehr speziell. Aber Wörter, die auf den letzten beiden Seiten eines Kapitels wiederholt werden (*im Content and language workout*), die solltet ihr aktiv beherrschen.

 Hier bekommt ihr Tipps, wie ihr eine Aufgabe lösen könnt.

Enter the web-code GO310517–x. In diesem Heft werden viele Web-codes angegeben. Tragt sie auf der Seite www.cornelsen.de in das entsprechende Feld ein und ihr findet dort Materialien oder weiterführende Links.

Viel Spaß mit diesem Buch wünschen Euch
Heiner Böttger und Oliver Meyer

Scenario 1: From town to town

Getting started

A small town

Here's a song about a small town, but the parts are in the wrong order.

1. Listen to the song and put the parts in the right order.

Words

A
- *I've seen it all:* ich habe schon alles gesehen
- *had myself a ball:* hatte viel Spaß
- *married:* heiratete
- *l. a. doll:* ein Mädchen aus Los Angeles
- *brought:* brachte

B
- *was born:* wurde geboren
- *small:* klein
- *probably:* wahrscheinlich
- *die:* sterben
- *community:* Gemeinschaft

C
- *cannot:* can't
- *forget:* vergessen
- *who:* der/die/das
- *be myself:* ich selbst sein
- *let:* lassen

D
- *provides little opportunity:* bietet wenig Möglichkeiten

E
- *breathe:* atmen
- *gonna die:* werde sterben
- *where they'll bury me:* wo sie mich begraben werden

F
- *educated:* aufgezogen
- *taught:* gelehrt, beigebracht
- *fear:* Furcht
- *used to daydream:* hatte immer Tagträume

G
- *got* = *have got*
- *nothing:* nichts
- *hayseed:* Mensch vom Land

A) But I've seen it all in a small town
Had myself a ball in a small town
Married an l.a. doll and brought her to this small town
Now she's small town just like me

B) Well I was born in a small town
And I live in a small town
Probably die in a small town
Oh, those small communities.

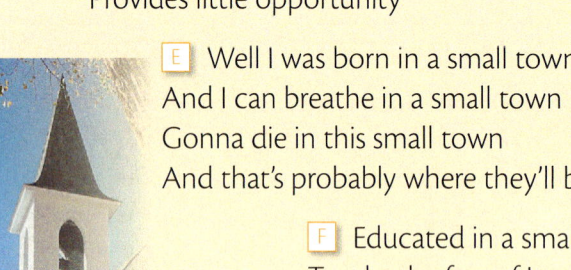

C) No I cannot forget where it is that I come from
I cannot forget the people who love me
Yeah, I can be myself here in this small town
And people let me be just what I want to be

D) All my friends are so small town
My parents live in the same small town
My job is so small town
Provides little opportunity

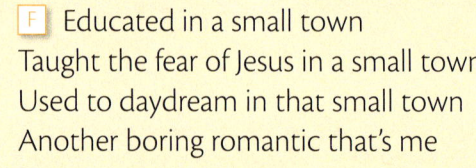

E) Well I was born in a small town
And I can breathe in a small town
Gonna die in this small town
And that's probably where they'll bury me

F) Educated in a small town
Taught the fear of Jesus in a small town
Used to daydream in that small town
Another boring romantic that's me

G) Got nothing against a big town
Still hayseed enough to say
Look who's in the big town
But my bed is in a small town
Oh, and that's good enough for me   (music and lyrics: John Mellencamp)

2. Read the song again and try to understand as much as you can.

3. Make two lists: What does the singer love about small towns? What does he not like about small towns? Write down three things in each list.

4. Enter the web-code GO310517–4 and watch the video.
   A) List five more things about small town life.
   B) Describe your hometown . Is it like in the video? What do you like about it? What do you not like about it?

Words
- *map:* Karte

5. Make a map of your ideal  town and present it to the others.

LAT Memorizing

Getting to Nuremberg

Words
- memorize: auswendig lernen
- south: Süden
- capital: Hauptstadt
- Franconian: fränkisch
- east: Osten
- hill: Hügel
- lake: See

1 Read one of the texts and memorize it. Then present it to your class.

1. Nuremberg is a city in Bavaria. Bavaria is in the south of Germany. Other cities in Bavaria are Augsburg, Regensburg and Bayreuth. The capital of Bavaria is Munich. The winters here are usually not very cold and the summers are usually sunny and warm.

2. Near Nuremberg there are a lot of interesting places to see. In the north there is the 'Franconian Switzerland' and in the east there are the Franconian hills. The Franconian lakes in the south-west are also not very far away. Erlangen and Fürth are cities near Nuremberg.

3. Nuremberg is a very big city. Half a million people live there. In the north of the city there is an airport and the harbour is in the south-west. The train station is in the city centre. Lots of tourists come to Nuremberg every year. They usually go shopping and walk around to see some sights.

Words
- half a million: eine halbe Million
- harbour: Hafen
- sight: Sehenswürdigkeit

2 When other pupils present their text, fill in the gaps.

Words
- fill in the gaps: die Lücken ausfüllen

A Nuremberg is a _____ in Bavaria.

B The winters here are usually _____ and the summers are usually sunny and warm.

C The Franconian lakes in the south-west are not very _____.

D _____ and Fürth are cities near Nuremberg.

E In the _____ of the city there is an airport and the harbour is in the south-west.

F The _____ is in the city centre.

Some German place names are different in English. Nuremberg = Nürnberg, Bavaria = Bayern. Can you guess what Munich, Cologne and Lake Constance are in German?

Scenario 1: From town to town

 LAT Productive listening

Find your way through Limburg

1. Your teacher tells you the way through Limburg. Take a coloured pen and mark the way on the map.

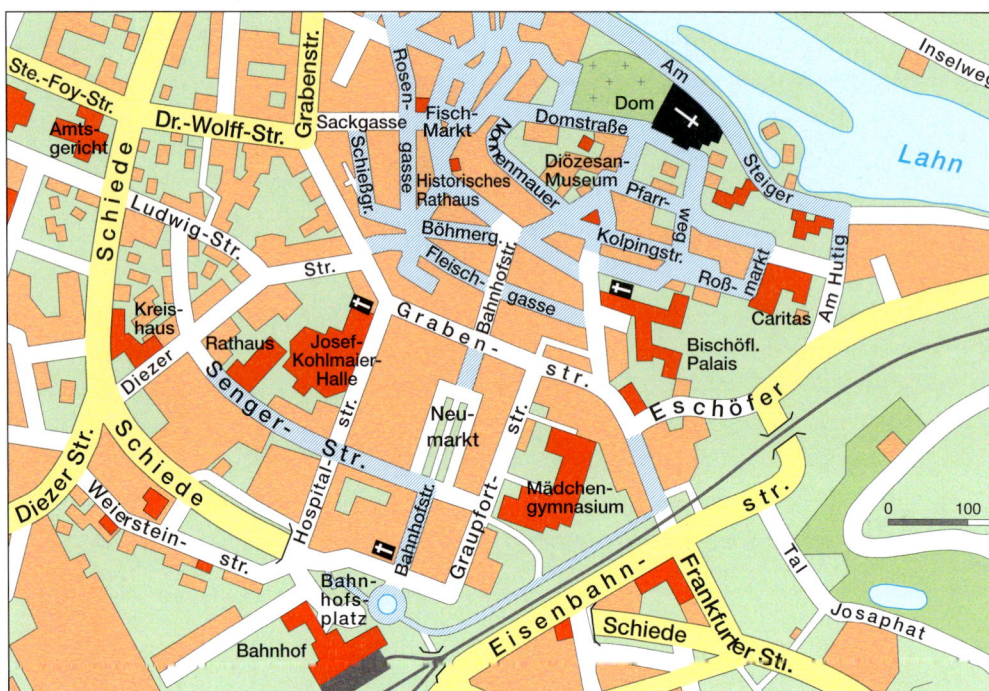

- start at …
- follow … Straße
- turn left/right (into … Straße)
- don't …
- go straight on (= geradeaus)
- walk along …

2. Now work out a tour for your classmates.

 LAT Working with pictures

What's where?

Look at this picture of Dresden.

1. Choose one of the four parts of the picture. What can you see? Take notes.

2. Describe your part of the picture. Your classmates guess what part you are talking about.

3. Bring your own picture to class and say what you can see.

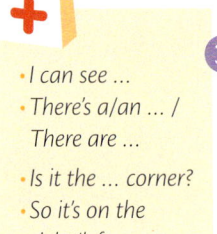

- I can see …
- There's a/an … / There are …
- Is it the … corner?
- So it's on the right/left.

6 Going CLIL

LAT Converting into language

In town

Was machen die Leute eigentlich so in der Stadt? In diesem Spiel kannst du es beschreiben.

Würfele mit zwei Würfeln. Die höhere Augenzahl gibt dir die Spalte in der Tabelle unten an, die niedrigere die Zeile.

Suche das richtige Feld in der Tabelle, lies die Stichworte und mache einen englischen Satz daraus. Ist er richtig? Dann gibt die kleine Ziffer in dem Feld an, wie viele Punkte du dafür bekommst. Natürlich gewinnt, wer am meisten Punkte hat!

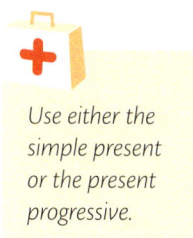

Use either the simple present or the present progressive.

down \ across	⚀	⚁	⚂	⚃	⚄	⚅
⚀	The statue / stand / in front of the museum. ④	The Toy Museum / open / at 10 am every day. ④	It's 6 o'clock, so Stephen / get up / right now. ⑥	Most people / like / Leipzig. ③	Tony / wait / at the *Museumsbrücke* at the moment. ③	What / you / do / at the moment? ③
⚁	There's Julie over there. She / text / Laura again. ⑤	Tina and Tim / play hockey every weekend. ②	School / start / at 8 o'clock every Monday. ②	The Rock Festival / be / always on the first weekend in May. ④	Every year lots of tourists / come / to see Berlin. ③	Now we / be / at the Industrial Museum. ④
⚂	Bus tours normally / start / at 9:30 pm. ③	Usually every tourist / buy / a T-shirt. ④	The Christmas market / be / always in December. ④	Jo often / go / to school by bike. ②	Sandie / not know / the way to the sports shop. ⑤	Asif sometimes / go / to the football stadium. ③
⚃	Right now Ananda / wait for / the train from Cologne. ③	Paul / just / take / a picture of the harbour. ⑥	Ivy never / drink / beer. ③	Susan / eat / ice cream right now. ③	I / go / skating every weekend. ④	Tina often / go / to the zoo with her aunt. ④
⚄	Dad / watch / the tennis match on TV. ⑤	My parents never / go / to town by car. ⑦	Our football team / play / very well this year. ⑤	My mum often / go / to the Classic Open Air. ④	Look! Jack / stand / there in front of the Cabot Tower. ⑦	A group of tourists / wait / in front of the museum. ③
⚅	Tony is over there. He / eat / a 'Pfannkuchen'. ⑥	Gemma / sit / in front of the library. ⑦	Jasmin often / see / her friends in the evening. ④	Daniel sometimes / eat / a hamburger after school. ⑥	Rose is over there. She / look / at us. ④	When she goes to school, Latisha / walk / along Broad Street. ④

Going CLIL

Scenario 1: From town to town

LAT Extracting meaning

Sightseeing

Many cities have great monuments . Bielefeld, for example, has the Sparrenburg Castle.

1 Read the text about Sparrenburg Castle. There are many words you can't understand. Don't worry – try to understand as much as you can.

Sparrenburg Castle

Sparrenburg Castle rises high above the city of Bielefeld. The counts of Ravensburg constructed it between 1240 and 1250. It has a high defensive wall and a tower with a height of 37m. Visitors can climb the tower and enjoy a great view over the town and the countryside. They can also explore the big system of underground passages – there are 285 m of tunnels under the earth! People say that there is even a secret tunnel from the castle to the city, but people don't know where it is exactly. You can only visit the northwestern part of the castle three times a year, as there are bats living there. During the Sparrenburgfest on the last weekend of July you feel like you are in the Middle Ages.

Words
- *above:* über
- *count:* Graf
- *view:* Aussicht
- *three times a year:* drei Mal pro Jahr
- *feel like:* sich fühlen als ob

2 Here are some difficult words from the text.
  A Guess their German meanings and write them down.
  B What helped you understand the words? Tick ✔ the right box.

	Bedeutung (auf Deutsch)	Bild	Zusammen-hang	ähnliches Wort*	Allgemein-wissen	anderes
castle						
to rise						
to construct						
defensive wall						
height						
passage						
secret						
visit						
bat						
Middle Ages						

*in Englisch, Deutsch oder anderen Sprachen

Scenario 1: From town to town

Content and language workout

Rounding off

1. **A treasure hunt**
Sieh dir den Stadtplan von Mainz an und überlege, wo du fünf kleine Schätze verstecken würdest.

Nun schick einen Mitspieler / eine Mitspielerin auf die Suche: Verbinde ihm/ihr die Augen und beschreibe (auf Englisch!) den Weg von einem Schatz zum nächsten. Er/Sie folgt deiner Wegbeschreibung mit dem Finger auf der Karte, bis der letzte Schatz gefunden ist. Stoppe seine/ihre Zeit. Welches Paar ist am schnellsten?

Words
- *treasure hunt*: Schatzsuche

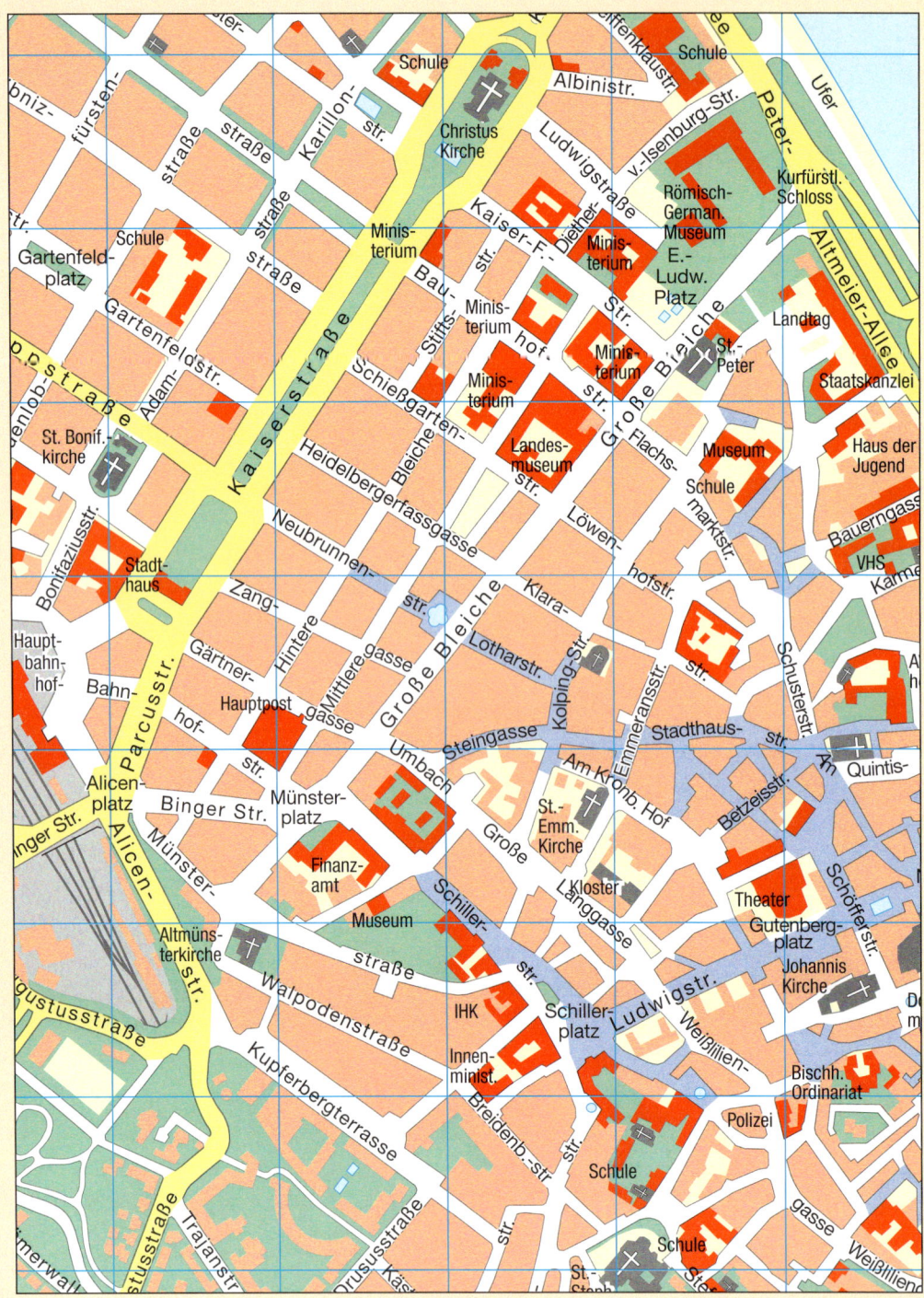

2 In English, please

Write down the English words:

Bayern _____

Nürnberg _____

München _____

Franken _____

3 All mixed up

The letters in these words are mixed up. Can you write them in the correct order?

tesa   tyci   palitca   lilh   alke   pirorat   rarbohu   ranit   atisont   recten   sghits

_____

_____

_____

_____

_____

_____

_____

Scenario 2: Where I come from

Getting started

A secret code

Can you crack the code and fill in the blanks?

A The *Rhein* is a ⬜✖❖✿⬜ ☐☐☐☐☐.

B A beach is always near the ◆✿➢◆✖♠♣ ☐☐☐☐☐☐☐☐.

C Germany is a big ●✣▼◗☐☆ ☐☐☐☐☐☐☐ in the middle of Europe.

D Berlin is the ●➢■✖◯➢✹ ☐☐☐☐☐☐☐ of Germany.

E Nuremberg is in Bavaria and Bavaria is in the ◆✣▼◯♥ ☐☐☐☐☐ of Germany.

F The sun 💡 rises in the ✿➢◆◯ ☐☐☐☐ and sets in the ✣✿◆◯ ☐☐☐☐.

G The Kilimanjaro and the Mount Everest are I✣▼◯➢✖◆ ☐☐☐☐☐☐☐☐☐.

H A ◯✣✣◗ ☐☐☐☐ is a place where many people live.

I On a I➢■ ☐☐☐ you can see the rivers, cities and mountains of a country.

J An ✖◆✹➢◗♠ ☐☐☐☐☐☐ is a piece of land in the middle 💡 of the sea.

K Asia and America are ●✣◗◯✖◗✿◯◆ ☐☐☐☐☐☐☐☐☐.

L The *Bodensee* is a ✹➢✿ ☐☐☐☐.

Words
- *secret code:* Geheimcode
- *beach:* Strand
- *rise:* aufgehen
- *set:* untergehen

Kilimanjaro

Mount Everest

an island

Lake Constance

| ♥ | ☆ | ◗ | ✿ | ■ | ✣ | ✹ | ➢ | ❖ | ▼ | ● | ◯ | ✖ | ◆ | ➢ | ♠ | ✣ | I | ⬜ |
| | | | | | | | | | | | | | | | | | | |

12 Going CLIL

LAT Converting into language

Cornwall calling

Paul from Nuremberg is planning to visit his friend Amy in St. Ives in Cornwall. Paul doesn't know Cornwall, so Amy sends him a map.

- There is a/an ... in ...
- In ... you can ...

1 Write ten sentences about Cornwall. Think of cities, rivers, mountains and the sea, but also of activities you can do there.

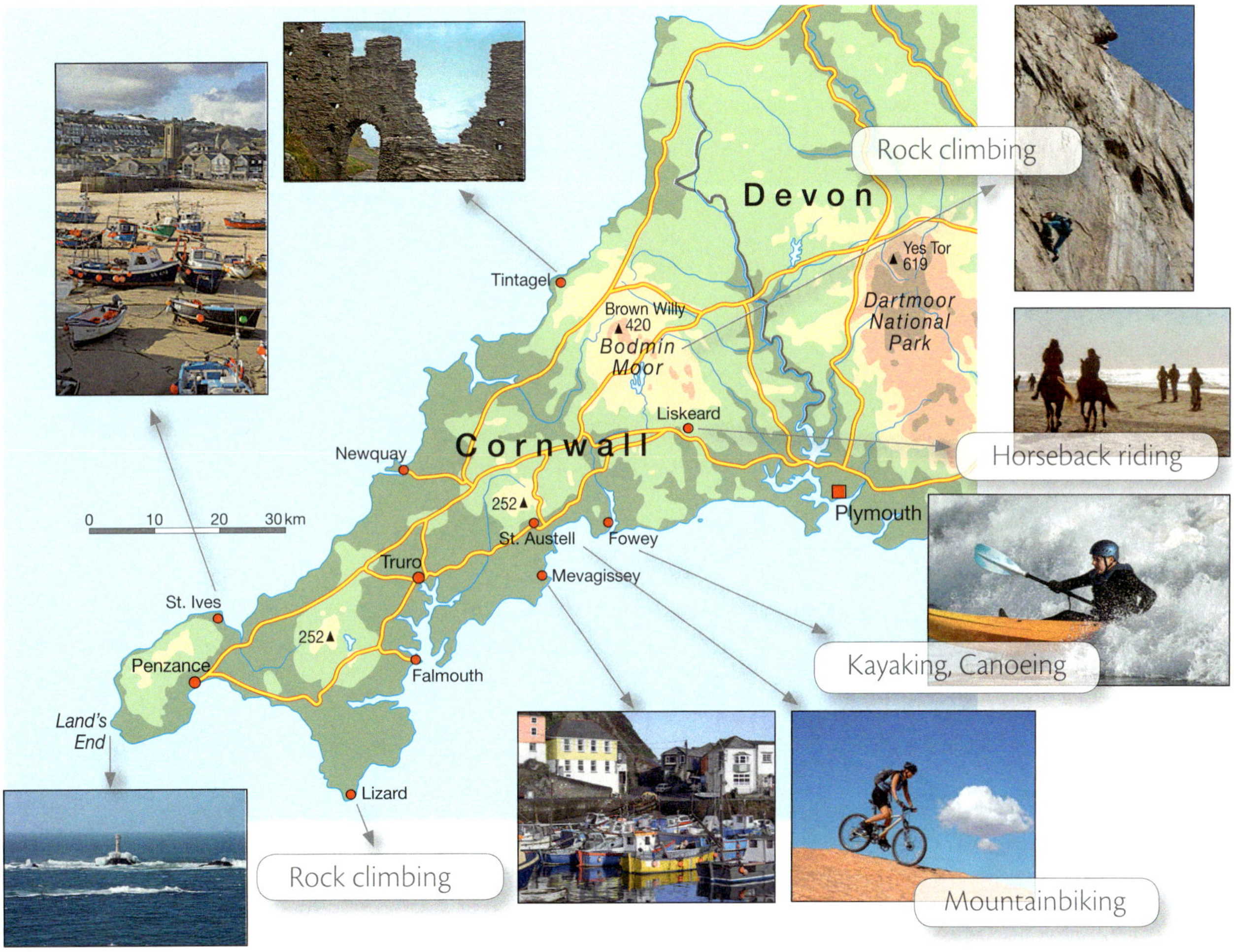

2 Paul is planning to stay in Cornwall for a week. He tells his friend Leon what he would like to do each day. Write down what he says.

Example

On Monday I would like to go canoeing.

| On | Monday
...
the second /third /
... / last day | I'd like to
I'd love to | go (to)
see
visit
take | horseback riding
rock climbing
fishing
surfing lessons
Penzance
the beach
... |

Scenario 2: Where I come from

Words
- *decide*: sich entscheiden
- *below*: unten

3 Now Paul has to decide when he wants to go to Cornwall. He calls Amy.
  a With a partner, act out Amy and Paul's dialogue.
     You work with the calendar below, your partner goes to p. 16. Find seven days when you can visit him or her.

Paul's calendar

Juli						
Mo	Di	Mi	Do	Fr	Sa	So
29	30	1	2	3	4	5
6	7	8	9	10	11	12
13	14	15	16	17	18 Ferienbeginn	19 Fußballturnier
20	21	22	23	24	25	26 Italien
27	28	29	30	31	1	2

August						
Mo	Di	Mi	Do	Fr	Sa	So
27	28	29	30	31	1	2
3	4	5	6	7	8	9
10	11	12	13	14	15 Kanuwochenende	16
17	18	19	20	21	22	23
24	25 Ferienende	26	27	28	29	30
31	1	2	3	4	5	6

Example

What about the week from the 8th to the 15th of July?

What about	the week from ... to ...?	Yes, that's fine.
What do you think of		No, I'm sorry, that's not possible. We're (in Italy) then.
Is	... to ...	ok? possible? fine with you?

Use your mobile phone to record the dialogue.

  b Record your dialogue. Correct it or ask your teacher to help you, then record it again.

 LAT Extracting meaning

Get active!

Paul wants to know more about activities in Cornwall. Enter the web-code GO310517–15 and click on the link that appears. Choose one activity. Then write Paul's e-mail to a friend and tell him or her about the activity (in German).

 LAT Productive listening

And where are you from?

Two months later, Paul is in St. Ives and meets Amy's friend Celina.

1. Listen to Paul and Celina talking.

2. Look at the following sentences. What does Paul say and what does Celina say? Write the right letters in the bubbles.

 A 'I live in Cardiff, the capital of Wales.'
 B 'I like canoeing on the Pegnitz.'
 C 'I love skiing in the mountains.'
 D 'In winter, I often go to Scotland.'
 E 'It often rains where I come from.'
 F 'My home town is in the south of Wales.'
 G 'My friends often go canoeing.'
 H 'Where I come from the sun often shines in summer.'

Words
- *canoeing*: Kanufahren

Scenario 2: Where I come from

LAT  Memorizing

Celina and Amy's home

One day, Celina and Amy show Paul a map of Britain. Work with a partner. One of you memorizes what Celina tells you and the other plays Amy's role.

Du darfst dir Stichwörter machen!

Celina:

Look, this is a map of Great Britain. Here's London. It's in the south-east and I'd love to live there. The River Thames flows through it. Edinburgh is a city in the north-east of Britain, in Scotland. South of Edinburgh, the River Tweed flows.

Amy:

Great Britain is mostly flat but in the north and west we have some mountains. Ben Nevis is the highest mountain in Great Britain. It's in Scotland and it's 1343m high. My parents and I go there for a holiday sometimes. You can even go skiing in Scotland.

Words
- *I'd love to:* ich würde sehr gerne
- *flow through:* fließen durch
- *mostly flat:* meist flach
- *highest:* höchste/r, s

LAT Converting into language, task 3 (cf. p. 14)

July				
We	1	Th	16	
Th	2	Fr	17	
Fr	3	Sa	18	
Sa	4	Su	19	
Su	5	Mo	20	
Mo	6	Tu	21	First day of the holidays
Tu	7	We	22	
We	8	Th	23	
Th	9	Fr	24	
Fr	10	Sa	25	
Sa	11	Su	26	
Su	12	Mo	27	
Mo	13	Tu	28	Off to Conil!
Tu	14	We	29	
We	15	Th	30	
		Fr	31	

Amy's calendar

August				
Sa	1	Su	16	
Su	2	Mo	17	
Mo	3	Tu	18	See Linda
Tu	4	We	19	
We	5	Th	20	
Th	6	Fr	21	
Fr	7	Sa	22	
Sa	8	Su	23	
Su	9	Mo	24	
Mo	10	Back from Conil!	Tu	25
Tu	11		We	26
We	12		Th	27
Th	13		Fr	28
Fr	14		Sa	29	Julian's wedding
Sa	15		Su	30	Last day of the holidays
			Mo	31

LAT Working with pictures

Presenting Bavaria

Of course, Celina and Amy want to know about Bavaria where Paul comes from. Use the words from the boxes to fill in the gaps below.

| Bavaria | south-east | Zugspitze | Pegnitz |
| north | map | south | Nuremberg |

And this is a _____ of _____, where I come from. Munich is in the _____ and I'd just love to live there. The River Donau flows through Bavaria. _____ lies in the north of Bavaria. The River _____ flows through Nuremberg. Bavaria is mostly flat but in the _____ we have some mountains. _____ is a mountain in the south. My parents and I sometimes go there.

Scenario 2: Where I come from

Content and language workout

Rounding off

1 All maps normally have the following elements 💡:

Title

Scale line ①

Compass ②

Key ③

Elevation ④

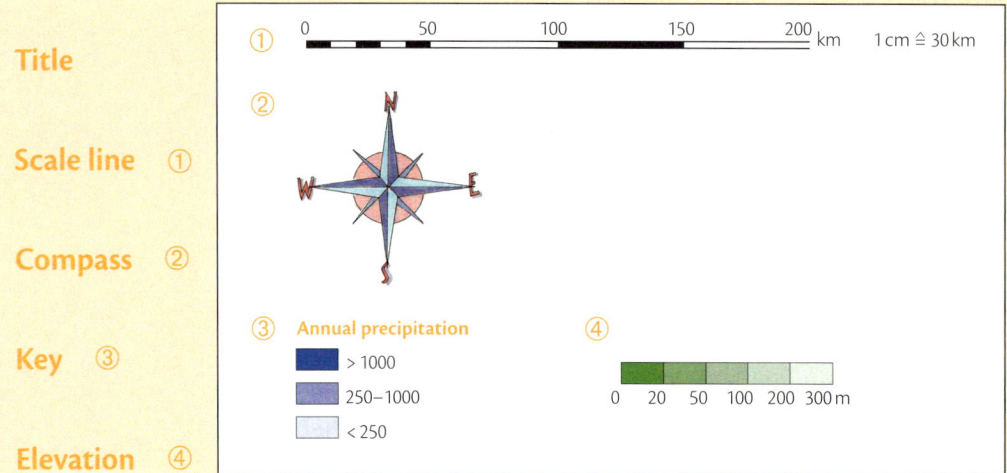

Match these English words to their definitions and fill in the German word.

Here are the German words:
- *Legende*
- *Maßstab*
- *Titel*
- *Kompassrose*
- *Höhe über Null*

English word	Definition	German word
_____	It tells you how long a centimetre 💡 on the map is in reality.	_____
_____	It tells you what the symbols 💡 on a map mean.	_____
_____	It tells you what the map shows.	_____
_____	It tells you where north is on a map.	_____
_____	It tells you how high a place is.	_____

Words
- *high:* hoch

Going CLIL

2 Was ist spannend an der Region, in der du lebst? Zeichne eine Karte für Freunde, die sie nicht kennen. Trage (auf Englisch!) alle Dinge ein, die du für wichtig hältst – und vergiss nicht Sport und Spaß! Denk daran, alle Elemente aufzunehmen, die Karten normalerweise haben (vgl. Aufgabe 1).

3 Present your map to the class. Here are some phrases:

> This is a map of …
>
> On the map you can see …
>
> The map shows … (a country/city / rivers/mountains)
>
> In the centre / in the middle of the map there is …
>
> A river flows through …
>
> … lies in the south/north/east/west.
>
> … is/lies/flows south/north/west/east of …
>
> In … you can …

Scenario 3: When in Rome …

Getting started

Are you a real expert?

Fill in the blanks. You can find the words in the maze under the text.
The numbers on the right tell you how many points you get for a correct answer.

1	English word for 'Rom':	_____ 1
2	Name of the river in the city:	_____ 2
3	Name for politicians in the Roman Empire:	_____ 2
4	Bridge that transports water:	_____ 3
5	'Mother' of Romulus and Remus:	*a*_____ 2
6	Roman god of war:	_____ 2
7	Famous Roman ruler:	_____ 2
8	Commander who fought the Romans with elephants:	_____ 2

Words
- *blank*: Lücke
- *maze*: Labyrinth, Labyrinthrätsel
- *politician*: Politiker/in
- *god of war*: Kriegsgott
- *ruler*: Herrscher
- *commander*: Befehlshaber
- *fight, fought, fought*: (be)kämpfen

Total: ____ / 16

Score

16–14 points:
Are you sure you're not Roman?

13–11 points:
Well done!

10–8 points:
Not bad.

7–5 points:
You can learn lots of new things here.

5–0 points:
The Romans aren't really your strong point, are they?

```
H  A  N  N  I  B  A  L  E
O  T  S  E  I  N  Q  U  A
R  T  O  O  W  A  U  M  L
M  I  R  R  O  M  E  L  T
A  G  C  I  L  E  D  R  I
N  E  A  L  F  R  U  V  B
G  R  E  T  E  R  C  H  E
E  R  S  E  N  A  T  O  R
L  E  A  N  P  L  U  T  O
M  A  R  S  U  E  S  A  S
```

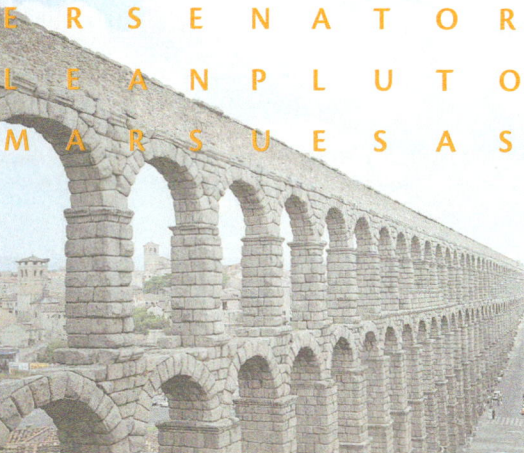

Are you finished?
There are some more words in the maze. Can you find five of them?

_____
_____
_____
_____
_____

20 Going CLIL

LAT Working with pictures

Where are they?

1 Where are they in this picture of ancient Rome: a senator, a pillar, a group of people, a horse, some clouds. Complete the sentences below.

Fill in
- in the middle
- in the foreground
- in the background
- at the top
- at the bottom
- on the left/right
- in the top/bottom corner
- in the left/right corner

left corner	top	right corner
left	middle	right
left corner	bottom	right corner

Example

There is a statue _in the middle._ _____

A In this picture there is a group of people _____.

B A senator is standing _____. He is wearing a toga.

C There's a horse _____.

D _____ there is a pillar.

E There are clouds _____.

Words
- *ancient*: alt, antik
- *pillar*: Säule
- *cloud*: Wolke

Scenario 3: When in Rome …

2 Look at the picture again. Can you find the people below? Answer the questions.

a Where are the people in the picture?
b What do they look like and what clothes are they wearing?
c What are they doing at the moment?

a The man is _____

b _____

c _____

a _____

b _____

c _____

a _____

b _____

c _____

Words
- the fewest questions: die wenigsten Fragen

3 Choose one of the people in the picture. Ask your partner questions to find out which person he/she is thinking about. The pupil with the fewest questions wins.

4 Sieh dir die Kleidung der Personen noch einmal genau an. Was sagt sie dir über die Stellung der Personen in der Gesellschaft?

LAT Productive listening

On Marcus's heels

In the year 397 AD young Marcus came to the ancient city of Rome. He wanted to find his aunt's house.
Your teacher now tells you which way he went. Take a coloured pen and mark his way on the map.

Words
- on Marcus's heels: auf Marcus' Fersen

Scenario 3: When in Rome …

LAT Converting into language

What happened?

1 Do you remember what Marcus did on his journey?
Make sentences in the simple past. Then put the sentences in the correct order and write the numbers in the boxes.

Example		
Marcus / (to) ask / a centurion the way	Marcus asked a centurion the way.	1

Words
- *centurion:* Zenturio, Anführer einer Hundertschaft
- *cross:* überqueren

A The merchant / (to) send / Marcus to the Forum Romanum

B Marcus / (to) pass / the Aqueduct

C The centurion / not (to) know / where Via Cornelia is

D Marcus / (to) cross / the Tiber

E The senator / (to) explain / the rest of the way to Marcus

F He / (to) send / Marcus to the Colosseum

2 When Marcus got to his aunt's house, he told her about his day: what buildings he passed, who he met and what happened.

LAT Memorizing

Two dialogues

1 Work with a partner. Choose one of the dialogues 💡 and learn it. Then perform it in front of the class.

Words
- *perform:* darstellen, aufführen
- *chariot race:* Wagenrennen
- *lion:* Löwe

Dialogue A

Marcus gets to Rome

Marcus: Oh dear, I have no idea where to go. Excuse me, where am I?

Centurion: You are on Via Appia and there is the Circus Maximus. We have our chariot races there.

Marcus: Well, I'm looking for my aunt's house. She lives in Via Cornelia.

Centurion: Sorry, I don't know the street. But go to the Colosseum, where the gladiators 💡 fight against lions. You may find help there.

24 Going CLIL

Dialogue B

Marcus meets a merchant

Marcus: Hello. I'm looking for Via Cornelia. Can you help me, please?
Merchant: Yes, I can. Can you see the big buildings on the left? That's the Forum Romanum, the city's centre. Ask for the way when you're there.
Marcus: Thank you very much.
Merchant: You're welcome.

2 Write down two questions about your dialogue and ask your classmates.

Example

Where is Marcus?

_____

_____

LAT

The gladiators

1 This is the year 2567 and time travel is normal. You are travelling to ancient Rome because you want to collect material about gladiators for an exhibition. Get together in groups and work on *one* of the following tasks. Enter the web-code `GO310517–25` for useful links.

Words
- *time travel:* Zeitreise
- *exhibition:* Ausstellung
- *task:* Aufgabe
- *equipment:* Ausstattung
- *barracks:* Kaserne

a Write an interview with a gladiator (no more than one page). Find out how he became a gladiator, about his training and equipment, his life in the barracks and what it is like to fight in the Colosseum.
b Find out what happened in the Colosseum at a gladiator fight. Make a picture or describe the Colosseum.
c Find out about women gladiators. Write a short story or make a picture book about their lives.
d Choose your own topic and then collect and present information about it. Before you start to work, speak to your teacher about your topic.

2 Do you think you can trust the websites? Give reasons – in German if you like.

3 Which three things about gladiators surprised you most?

_____

_____

_____

Scenario 3: When in Rome …

Content and language workout

Rounding off

1. What can you see in the pictures? Write the words in the boxes.
   You can find the words in the maze on page 27.

   A In the picture there are two _____.
   Their equipment:

   _____ 💡 (German: _____)

   _____ 💡 (German: _____)

   _____ 💡 (German: _____)

   B This picture shows

   a _____ race

   in the _____ .

   C Below there is an aerial photograph (German: _____)
   of modern Rome.

   D On the right there is a _____

   of _____ Rome (ca. 44 BC).

   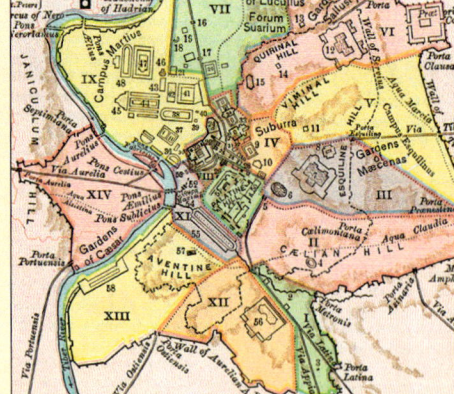

26 Going CLIL

E Here you can see a _____.

He is wearing a _____

In the picture *there* is a market.
Auf dem Bild *ist* ein Markt.

F In this picture there is a market.

_____ are selling their products.

```
R O M E R G I L S C P
S A N D A L S I N H A
E N S E N A T O R A N
M C H A R D A N O R T
R I N S H I E L D I H
M E R C H A N T S O E
A N F I L T O G A T L
P T C O L O S S E U M
F I S W O R D M K B E
C I R C U S S I E A T
```

2 Three extra words are in the maze. Can you find them?

_____

Scenario 4: Off to Europe

Getting started

Looking at Europe

1. Which European countries are they? Careful: The pictures do not show the right sizes.

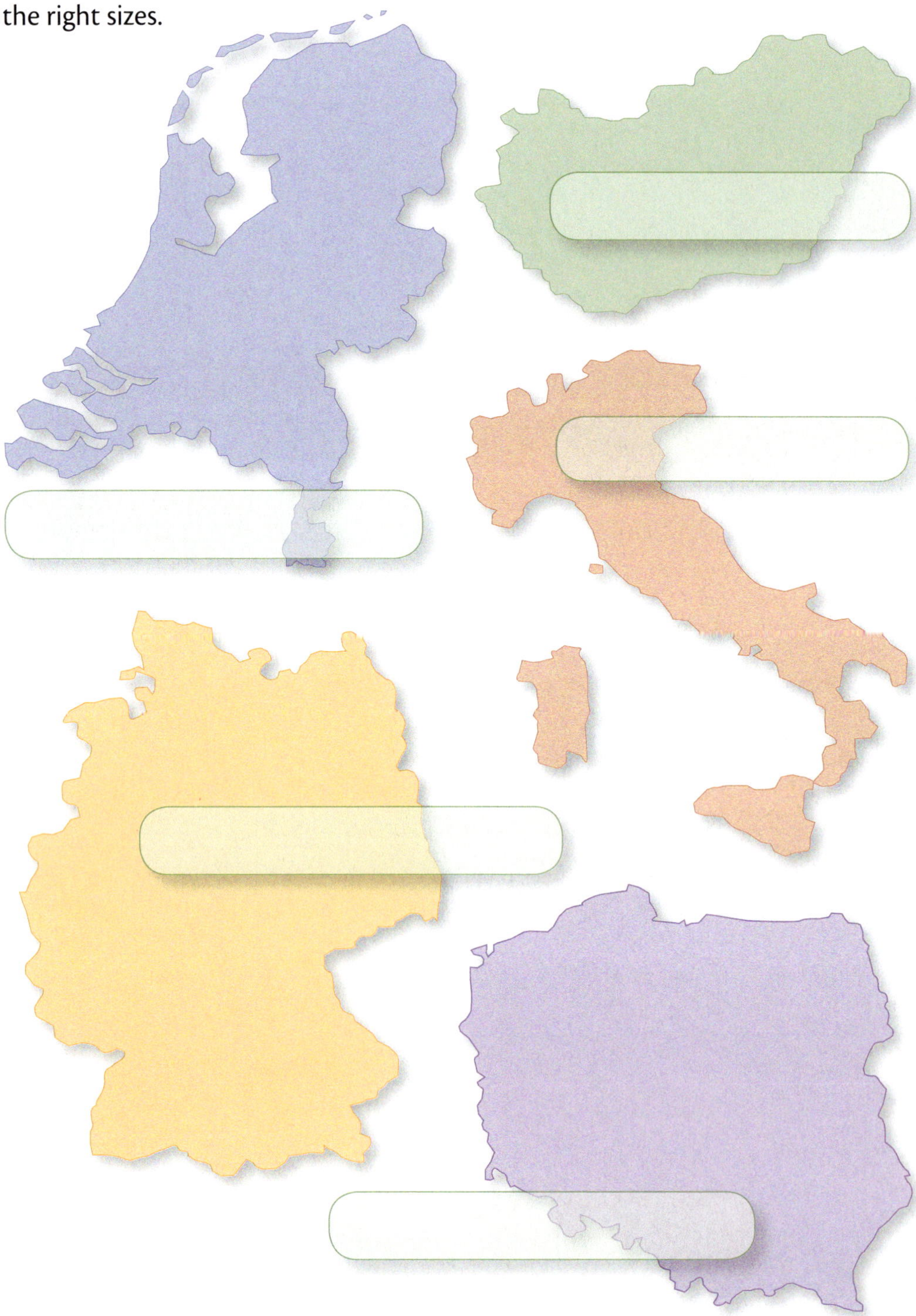

Start like this:
The most popular country is …,
the second most …,
the least popular …

2. Do an interview with two classmates.
   a Ask them the following questions and take notes: Which European country do you like best? Why?
   b Report your findings to the class.
   c Make a ranking of the countries in your class and present your results.

Words
- *ranking:* Rangfolge

28 Going CLIL

LAT Working with pictures

Images of Europe

The following pictures each show a cliché about a European country.

Words
- *clue:* Hinweis

1. Which countries do you think are in the pictures? Which clues helped you to decide?

2. List the clichés about the different countries.

3. Do you think it is important to know where the artist is from? Give reasons – in German, if you like.

LAT Productive listening

Comparing Europe

Listen to the text your teacher plays to you. Then do the following tasks:

Words
- *the right order:* die richtige Reihenfolge

1. Which is bigger? Put the following countries or regions in the right order. Start with the smallest.

   ☐ Australia   ☐ China   ☐ Europe   ☐ Germany   ☐ Japan

2. True or false? Tick ✓ the correct box.
   A Circa 82 million people live in Germany.   ☐ True   ☐ False
   B Circa 150 million people live in the USA. ☐ True   ☐ False
   C Circa 25 million people live in Europe.   ☐ True   ☐ False

Scenario 4: Off to Europe

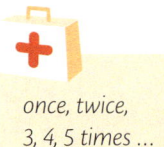

once, twice, 3, 4, 5 times …

3 'The Volga is three times longer than the Rhine'. What's that in German?

_____

4 Write down what these numbers refer to. You may use German.

Words

- *refer to*: sich beziehen auf

4,748: _____

40,000: _____

10.45: _____

8,850: _____

5 From what you now know about the following events, create a poster for one of them:

Tomato Battle

Periwinkle Spitting

Toe-Down Competition

Pig Festival

LAT Converting into language

Travelling to Europe

On p. 31 there is a table with the number of tourists in different European countries between 1995 and 2006. But it is not complete.

Work in pairs. Partner A should work with the table below; Partner B should go to p. 33 and find a table with the missing information there.

Partner A		Millions of foreign tourists				
Rank (2005)	Nation	1995	2000	2004	2005	2006 (provisional)
1st	France		77.2	75.1		79.1
2nd	Spain				55.9	58.5
5th	Italy	31.1	41.2	37.1	36.5	
6th	United Kingdom			25.7		30.1
7th	Germany	14.8	19.0		21.5	
9th	Austria		18.0	19.4		
11th	Turkey					18.9

based on: www.unwto.org/facts/eng/pdf/barometer/unwto_barom07_2_en.pdf

a Together, choose one country and make a chart about the number of tourists in this country. Your partner has the missing information.
b Describe your chart in five sentences. Why do you think the numbers are not the same every year?
c Fill in the blanks.

A The number of tourists who travelled to France rose sharply between 1995 and _____.

B The highest number of tourists arrived in Spain in _____.

C In _____ the lowest number of tourists arrived in Austria.

D The number of people who travelled to Turkey peaked in _____.

E In 2006, almost four times as many tourists stayed in _____ than in _____.

F The number of people who went to Italy increased between _____ and _____.

G Between 2000 and _____, the number of tourists in Italy dropped steadily.

H In Turkey, the number of tourists fell between _____ and 2005.

Charts

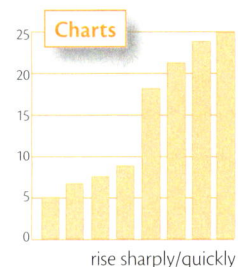
rise sharply/quickly

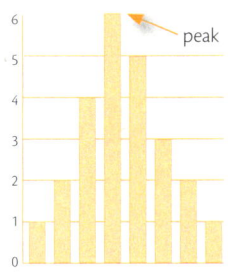
peak

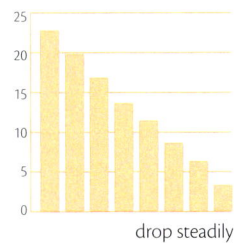
drop steadily

Words
- *highest number*: größte Anzahl
- *lowest number*: geringste Anzahl
- *four times as many*: vier Mal so viele
- *increase*: wachsen, steigen

Going CLIL **31**

Scenario 4: Off to Europe

 Extracting meaning

Words

- *crumpled up*: zerknüllt
- *unfold*: auseinanderfalten
- *spy*: Spion

Paris crumpled up

Your teacher will give you a crumpled up piece of paper with a text about Paris. You will be able to see many, but not all of the words in the text.

1. Try to guess the missing words and write the whole text down. You may not unfold the paper ball, but you may send spies to other groups to see what they have found out.

2. When you have finished, fill in the right words in the gaps.

A Paris: the _____ of France

B This number of people live in Paris: _____

C Another name for Paris: _____

D A famous museum in Paris: _____

E He painted the Mona Lisa: _____

F A famous tower: _____

G The river in Paris: _____

H A famous cathedral: _____

I A district with many painters and cafés: _____

32 Going CLIL

LAT Memorizing

A European exchange

Jonas Schmidt from Nuremberg has just arrived in Rome. He is on a school exchange with the Liceo Leonardo da Vinci in Rome. His exchange partner Giovanni Deollato welcomes him. With a partner, memorize and present the dialogue.

Dialogue

Giovanni: Hi, are you Jonas?
Jonas: Yes, I am.
Giovanni: Hello Jonas, I'm Giovanni. Welcome to Rome. How are you?
Jonas: I'm fine, thank you. How are you?
Giovanni: Great! Look, my mother's over there, by the car. My father is making some pasta for you at home.
Jonas: Mmm. I love pasta! I have got a CD for you. You wrote in your last e-mail that you like 'Tokio Hotel'.
Giovanni: Awesome! Thanks a lot. If you like, we can listen to some Italian rock music after dinner.
Jonas: Brilliant! Have you already made plans for the weekend?
Giovanni: Yes, we can do some sightseeing, for example at the Forum Romanum or the Colosseum.
Jonas: Good idea!
Giovanni: Glad you like it. OK then, let's go!

LAT Converting into language

Travelling to Europe (cf. p. 30)

Partner B						
Rank (2005)	Nation	1995	2000	2004	2005	2006 (provisional)
1st	France	60.0			75.9	
2nd	Spain	34.9	47.9	52.4		
5th	Italy					41.1
6th	United Kingdom	21.7	23.2		28.0	
7th	Germany			20.1		23.6
9th	Austria	17.2			20.0	20.3
11th	Turkey	7.1	9.6	16.8	20.3	

based on: www.unwto.org/facts/eng/pdf/barometer/unwto_barom07_2_en.pdf

Scenario 4: Off to Europe

Content and language workout

Rounding off

1. Fill in the gaps to describe the charts below. The following jumbled words may help you:

lafl	deasti-ly
cereased	cuqik-ly
sire	swol-ly
cinserea	prsah-ly

Example

The numbers rise steadily.

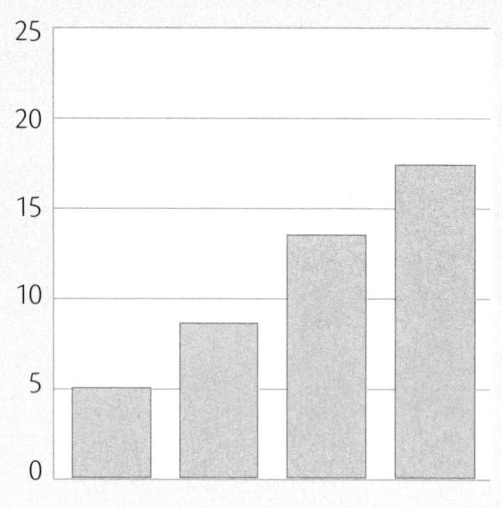

A The numbers _____ _____.

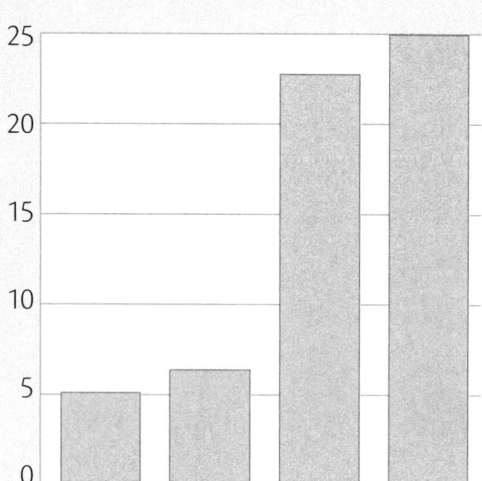

B The numbers _____ _____.

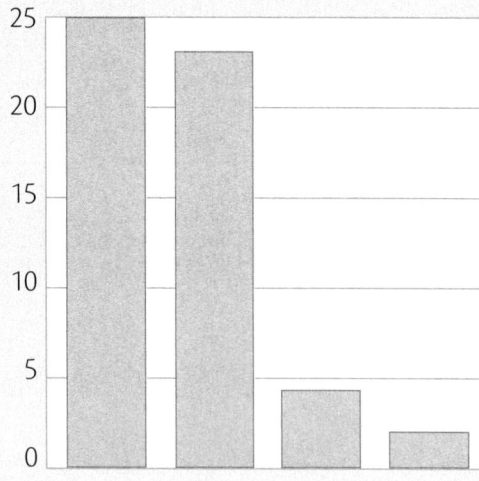

C The numbers _____ _____.

D The numbers _____ _____.

34 Going CLIL

2 Match the phrases and pictures.

three times as many: _____

the minimum / lowest number: _____

the maximum / highest number: _____

numbers peak: _____

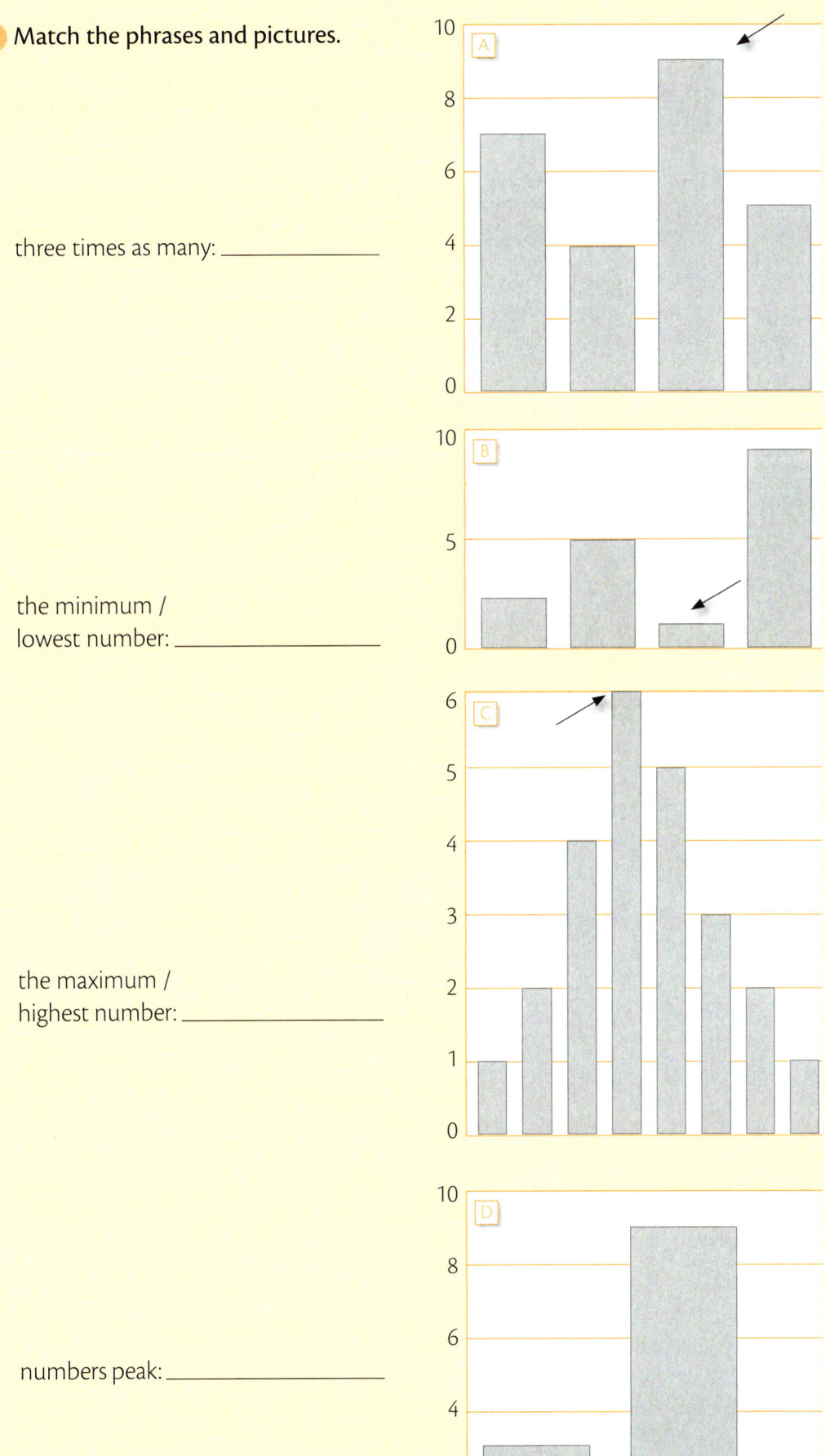

Scenario 5: Stormy weather ahead

Getting started

Going places in the British Isles

In the British Isles it usually rains a lot. Before you learn more about British weather, find out how well you know the geography of the British Isles.

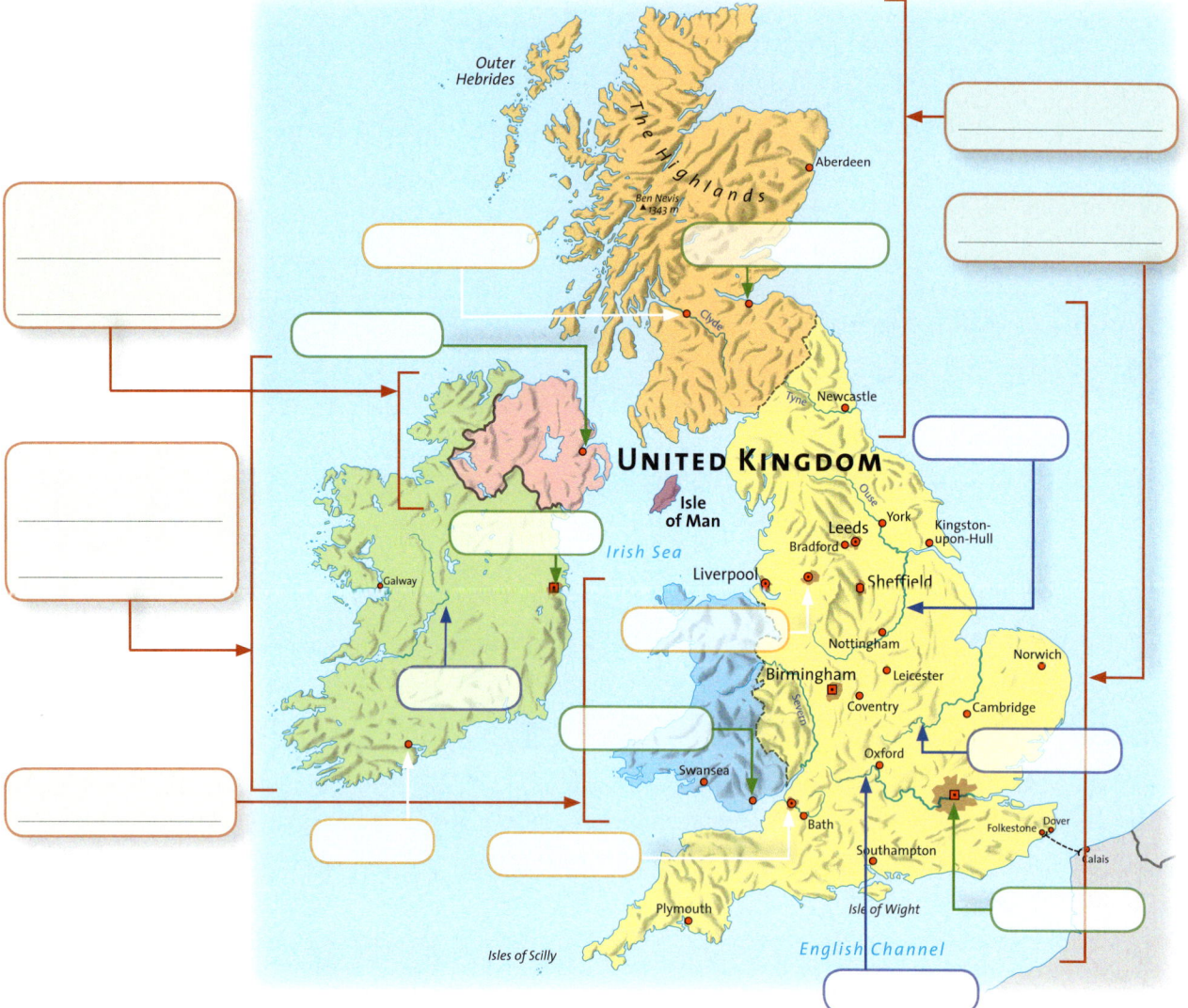

1 Write the names below in the boxes in the map.

Countries	Rivers	Capitals	Cities
England Northern Ireland Republic of Ireland Scotland Wales	Ouse Shannon Thames Trent	Belfast Cardiff Dublin Edinburgh London	Bristol Cork Glasgow Manchester

2 Work together with a partner. Think of a river or city in the British Isles and tell your partner where it is. Your partner has to guess its name.

Example

It's a river in the south of England. – The Thames.

LAT Memorizing

And now, the weather forecast for tomorrow

1 Work in groups of three. Your teacher will tell you which text you should work on. In your group, prepare a presentation of your weather forecast:

a   Read your text and make sure you understand it. These pictures will help you. Use a dictionary if necessary.

1	2	3	4	5	6	7	8
drizzle	rain	heavy rain	wind	strong wind	storm	fog	clouds

b   Learn your text so that you can present it.
c   Your teacher will give you some cards with weather symbols 💡. Be prepared to use them to show on a map what the weather will be like.
d   One of you presents your weather forecast, another one shows the weather symbols and the third person helps both if necessary.

The London weather studio

Good evening, ladies and gentlemen. This is ___(Name)___ from the London weather studio. Let me give you an outlook on the weather conditions 💡 for the next few days in England. Tomorrow the day will start warmer and brighter than in the last few days. Fewer clouds than yesterday will make for lots of sunny spells. Around noon we expect to have the sunniest hours of the day, with temperatures around 18°C. Later in the afternoon clouds will come in from the west and it will be as rainy as today. For the rest of the week, the weather conditions will get better, with more sun, less rain and higher temperatures.

Now let's go over to my colleague 💡 ___(Name)___ from the weather studio in Cardiff.

Words
- *outlook on:* Ausblick auf
- *few:* wenig
- *sunny spell:* sonniger Abschnitt
- *noon:* Mittag
- *expect:* erwarten
- *less:* weniger

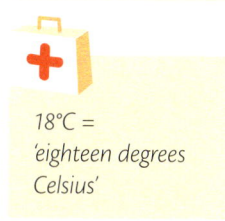

18°C = 'eighteen degrees Celsius'

The Cardiff weather studio

Noswaith dda! And here's the latest weather update from Wales with ___(Name)___. Here on the west coast it is wetter and windier than in England, with spells of heavy rain.
Last night Cardiff was the windiest place in the United Kingdom with very strong storms. The wind was stronger than in last winter's storms. In Wales the temperatures are now between 8 and 10°C, but they will go up and later it will be as warm as in England. Generally, it will become drier and brighter in the next couple of days.
With an update on the weather in the northern part of the country, here's ___(Name)___ from the weather studio in Edinburgh.

Words
- *Noswaith dda:* (Walisisch) Guten Abend!
- *spell of heavy rain:* Abschnitte mit starkem Regen
- *dry:* trocken
- *couple of days:* ein paar Tage

Scenario 5: Stormy weather ahead

Words
- *light:* leicht
- *however:* hingegen
- *expect:* erwarten
- *heavy rainfall:* starker Regenfall
- *light shower:* leichter Schauer
- *rise:* steigen

The Edinburgh weather studio

Good evening from up here in Scotland! This is _____(Name)_____ reporting. Here in Scotland we have had a bright day and it was drier than in England and Wales with just a few light showers. In the Highlands, however, temperatures were the coldest in the whole of the British Isles. On some mountains, like Ben Nevis, some snow even fell. Tomorrow we are expecting more and more clouds from Northern Ireland; they will bring the heaviest rainfalls we have seen so far this year.
Fog, drizzle and showers will dominate 💡 the weather in the coming days. Temperatures won't rise above 12°. So as always the weather is worst in Scotland. Good bye and good night to all our viewers in the UK and everywhere else.

2 Work in pairs. Put the weather symbols on a map to make your own weather forecast. Your partner must say what the weather will be like.

LAT ○○○ Converting into language

Weather by numbers

Words
- *per:* pro
- *mean annual temperature:* Jahresdurchschnittstemperatur

	Mean annual temperature		Rainfall wet days per year	Sun hours per year
	Winter	Summer		
Cardiff	7,2 °C	15,8 °C	180	51
London	6,3 °C	16,4 °C	153	47
Belfast	5,8 °C	13,9 °C	213	41
Edinburgh	5,8 °C	13,2 °C	191	47

Compare the weather in the four cities. Write down 10 sentences.

Example

In summer Cardiff is colder than London.
In winter Cardiff is the warmest city.

(In summer/winter)	_____	is (not) as	warm/cold dry/wet sunny/cloudy	as	_____
	_____	is	warmer/colder drier/wetter sunnier/cloudier	than	_____

(In summer/winter)	_____	is the	warmest/ coldest/ …	city

LAT Working with pictures

Rain in may

The following map shows you how much rain falls per year in the British Isles.

a Describe the map. Say what the colours mean.
b Explain what you have learned about rainfall in the British Isles.

Mean annual precipitation

- over 2000 mm
- under 2000 mm
- under 1500 mm
- under 1000 mm
- under 800 mm
- under 600 mm

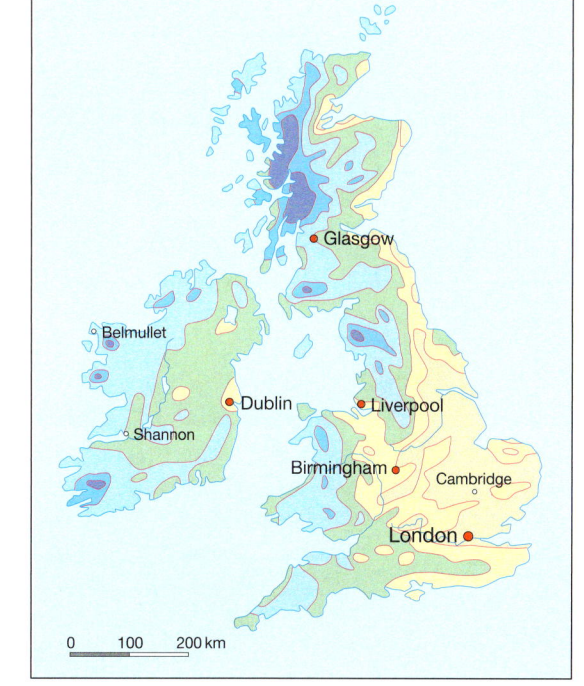

Scenario 5: Stormy weather ahead

LAT Productive listening

Palm trees in Ireland?

1 Lisa and her older brother Dylan live in York, in the north-east of England. They are talking about the climate.

   a First look at this word list and the pictures. They will help you to understand some of the difficult words in the dialogue that you will hear.

Word list
- pen pal: Brieffreund/in
- influence: beeinflussen
- mirror: Spiegel
- sunray: Sonnenstrahl
- store: speichern
- battery: Batterie
- Gulf Stream: Golfstrom
- current: Strömung
- scientist: Wissenschaftler/in
- global warming: globale Erderwärmung
- ice age: Eiszeit
- glacier: Gletscher
- melt: schmelzen
- freshwater: Süßwasser
- salt water: Salzwasser
- dense: dicht
- conveyor belt: Fließband

a polar bear

a camel in the desert

a sunflower

palm trees in Ireland

North Pole, *Siberia*, *the Alps*, *the equator*, *an ocean*

40 Going CLIL

b   Listen to the dialogue, then say whether the following statements are true or false. If they are false, correct them.

A   Mean annual temperatures are colder in the north than in the south of the earth. ☐ True ☐ False

B   Mountains do not influence the climate. ☐ True ☐ False

C   Near the ocean, the summers are warmer. ☐ True ☐ False

D   Near the ocean, winters are usually milder. ☐ True ☐ False

E   The Gulf Stream makes winters cold in Siberia. ☐ True ☐ False

2   Here's something for the real experts.

a   Listen again to the part about the Gulf Stream and put the pictures in the right order.

b   With the help of the pictures and the phrases below now describe what may happen to the Gulf Stream.

The Gulf Stream will come to a stop.

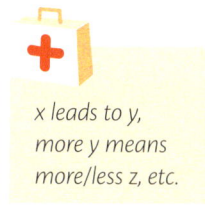

Less salt water: ocean water becomes less dense

Global warming: warmer temperatures

More ice melts; more fresh-water in the oceans

Salt water won't sink

x leads to y, more y means more/less z, etc.

Scenario 5: Stormy weather ahead

LAT Extracting meaning

Weird weather

If you think that snow in May is strange, read the following text and you'll see that the weather can be much weirder.

When you read the text, you'll probably think it is pretty difficult. Don't worry: You don't have to understand every word. You should rather try to find out the most important things even if there are unknown words. The tasks at the end will help you.

Weather can behave in some very strange ways. [...] Raining coal *(Say the word aloud)*, avalanches, giant hailstones and tornadoes are just some of the weird weather experiences that have hit southern England over the last century. We look at southern England's strangest meteorological moments.

"The Day After Tomorrow", USA, 2004, Regie: Roland Emmerich

Stormy weather

5 The great storm of 1958 in Sussex produced the biggest ever hailstones experienced in Britain. Stones the size of cricket balls fell on local people. There were also nearly 2,000 flashes of lightning in just one hour.
10 During the storm of June 1983 in Dorset, coke and coal fell out of the sky onto the hapless yachtsmen out for a pleasant day's sailing in Poole harbour. And the small village of Martinstown in Dorset also has its claim to fame. One day in July 1955 the tourists got a
15 lot more than they had asked for when the town experienced the heaviest ever rainfall to fall in one day in Britain.

Weird weather worldwide

Weird weather is a worldwide phenomenon. [...]
20 One of the weirdest happened in 1968 when southern England was covered by a shower of red dust. It was actually sand blown over 1,000 miles from the Sahara desert in Africa. It fell as red rain! Over the centuries there's been records of birds, frogs and other animals raining down from the skies. During a thunderstorm in 1939 in Wiltshire, the heavens opened and frogs fell on
25 local residents. Animal showers are often the result of small animals being sucked up by waterspouts, tornadoes and powerful updrafts. Even the Loch Ness Monster can be explained by weird weather. Small whirlwinds forming over warm waters can spin off a long tunnel funnel of water, looking like a sea monster.

Forecasting the weather

30 Before satellite weather pictures and weather forecasters, most people observed the weather for themselves, often using nature as their guide. So if you're trying to predict the weather in southern England, here's our guide to weather folklore.
Red sky at night – Shepherd's delight
Mare's tails – Storms and gales
35 Yellow sky at sunset – Wind in the morning
Mackerel sky – Never long wet, never long dry
Cows sitting down – Good chance of a downpour
Seabirds – Never good weather when birds are on sand
Quelle: http://www.bbc.co.uk/insideout/south/series1/weird-weather.shtml

Words
- *behave in strange ways:* sich merkwürdig verhalten
- *avalanche:* Lawine
- *hailstone:* Hagelkorn
- *meteorological:* das Wetter betreffend
- *the size of cricket balls:* mit der Größe von Kricketbällen
- *flash of lightning:* Blitz
- *coke:* Koks
- *sky:* Himmel
- *dust:* Staub
- *thunderstorm:* Gewitter
- *heavens opened:* der Himmel öffnete sich
- *suck up:* hinaufsaugen
- *waterspout:* Wasserhose
- *updraft:* Aufwind
- *whirlwind:* Wirbelsturm
- *observe:* beobachten
- *predict:* vorhersagen

1 Which of the following sentences best summarizes the first paragraph?
 A The weather can be very strange sometimes and this text will tell you more about it.
 B The weather in southern England and its people are strange.

2 What examples of strange weather does the first paragraph (ll. 1–4) give?

3 'Stones the size of cricket balls' (ll. 5–6): Which of the following phrases mean the same?
 A stones that are as big as cricket balls
 B stones that are bigger than cricket balls
 C stones that are not as big as cricket balls

4 Look at the sentence 'During the storm ...' (ll. 9–11). Try to decide what part of the sentence is most important. (If you do that first, you don't have to worry so much about the other parts of the sentence.)
 A 'during the storm of June 1983 in Dorset'
 B 'coke and coal fell out of the sky'
 C 'onto the hapless yachtsmen'
 D 'out for a pleasant day's sailing'
 E 'in Poole harbour'

5 In your own words, explain 'red rain' (l. 20) and 'animal showers' (cf. l. 21).

6 Which paragraphs of the text do the following pictures belong to? Describe what is happening.

7 Choose one of the weather proverbs (cf. ll. 33–38) and say what it means. You may need a dictionary.

Scenario 5: Stormy weather ahead

Content and language workout

Rounding off

1 Cool!
Put the words in the correct order. Start with the coldest temperature.

warm	hot
chilly	icy
cold	mild
cool	scorching

2 Fill in the verbs.

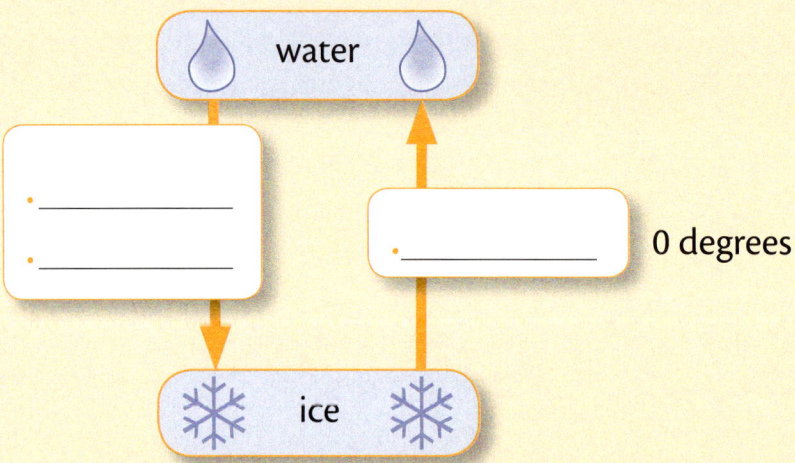

water

• _____
• _____

_____ 0 degrees

ice

3 Can you put these words in order? Make a mind map and group the words. You may need your dictionary.

breeze	drought	gust	moisture	shower	sunshine
cloud	dry	hail	muggy	sleet	tornado
cloudy	flood	heat	overcast	storm	typhoon
damp	fog	hurricane	precipitation	sun	wind
drizzle	gale	mist	rain	sunny	windy

climate

weather

44 Going CLIL

4 **What type of rain is it? Write the correct word under the pictures.**

A		B
	drizzle	
	gentle rain	
	heavy rain	
	light rain	
	pouring rain	

C	D	E

5 **There is no nasty weather, it's just a matter of the right clothing 💡! Match the pictures and the words.**

hood
rainproof jacket
hiking boots
sunglasses
sunblocker
gloves
umbrella

Going CLIL 45

Scenario 6: Of knights and ladies

Getting started

Winning the battle?

When we think of medieval times – or the Middle Ages – we often think of great battles.

1 Listen to a story about a famous battle in Britain, the Battle of Hastings (1066). Put the following pictures in the right order.

Words
- *battle:* Schlacht
- *medieval:* mittelalterlich
- *Middle Ages:* das Mittelalter (ca. 500–1500)

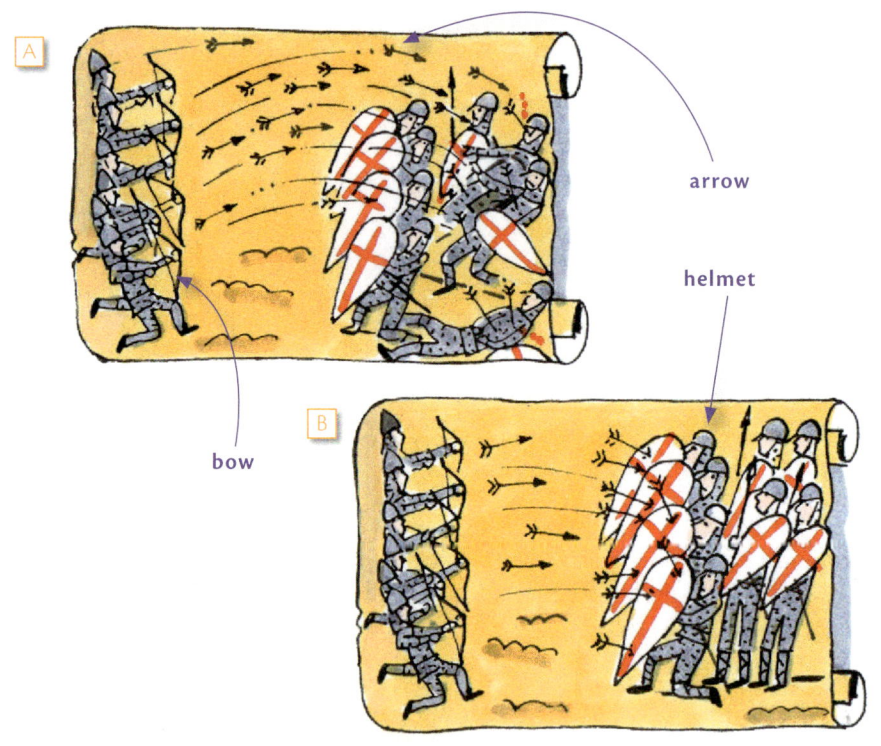

2 If you want to find out more about the Battle of Hastings, enter the web-code GO310517–46 for useful links.

46 Going CLIL

LAT Working with pictures

My home is my castle

1 At the beginning of the Middle Ages, most people lived in motte-and-baileys. Describe this picture of a motte-and-bailey.

Labels: chapel, huts, central tower, fence, motte, bridge, moat, bailey

2 Later in the Middle Ages, people made the motte-and-baileys larger. They turned them into castles.

  a Look at this picture of a castle and compare it to the motte-and-bailey. Find at least three things that have changed.
  b Compare your results with your neighbour. Add the things you missed.
  c Now write at least five sentences to describe how people have changed the motte-and-bailey.

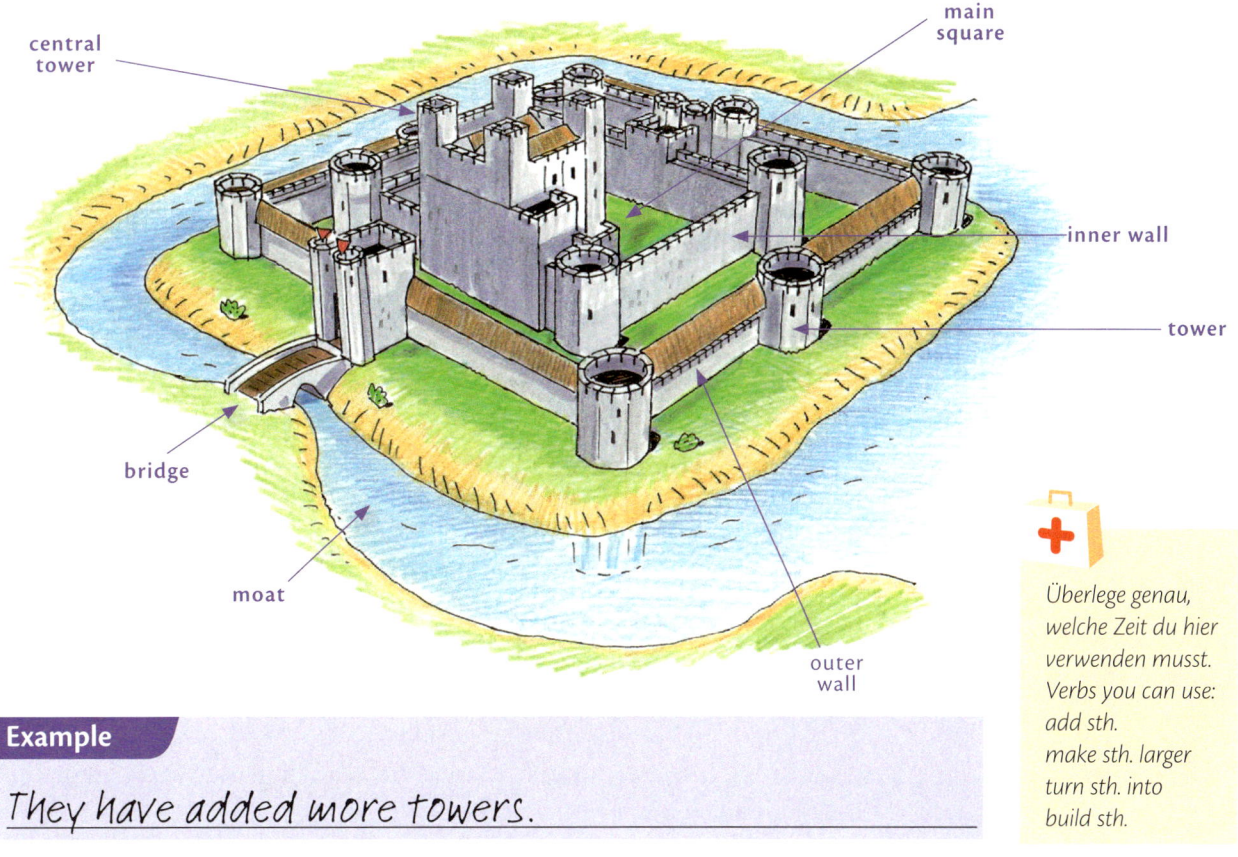

Labels: central tower, main square, inner wall, tower, bridge, moat, outer wall

> Überlege genau, welche Zeit du hier verwenden musst.
> Verbs you can use:
> add sth.
> make sth. larger
> turn sth. into
> build sth.

Example

They have added more towers.

  d Why do you think people made these changes?

Going CLIL **47**

Scenario 6: Of knights and ladies

LAT **Extracting meaning**

Growing up in medieval times

1 Find out how noble boys became knights and how girls became ladies.
   a   Work with a partner and decide who wants to read which of the texts below. Read the text carefully. Use a dictionary if necessary. Make notes.
   b   Tell your partner what you have found out. Make sure he or she understands.
   c   Swap roles. Take notes on what your partner tells you.
   d   Together, create a poster or a PowerPoint® presentation about knights and ladies. If you want more information, enter the web-code GO310 517–48 .

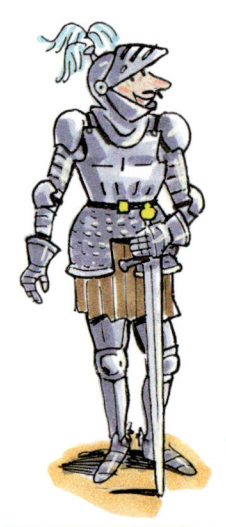

Becoming a knight

When a noble boy was seven years old, he went to live in the castle of another lord. There he began his education as a page. He learned good manners, how to read and write, numbers, how to sing, dance and play the lute, how to use a sword and
5   ride a horse. In the morning he helped his lord get dressed. He served at mealtimes and brought his master food and drink. Around the age of 13 the boy became the apprentice of a knight. From now on he was a squire. He had to learn how to fight with sword, lance and shield, and he learned the duties of a
10 knight. He looked after his master's horses, polished his weapons and armour and served him at mealtimes. When the squire grew older, he had to follow his master into battle and protect him there.
When the squire was ready to become a knight, usually between 
15 18 and 21, the knighting ceremony was held. On the night before the ceremony, the squire took a bath and took confession. He spent the whole night in the chapel and prayed to God. The next morning he put on white clothes and went into the crowded hall with his sword. The priest blessed the sword and then the squire knelt before his lord. The
20 lord then took the sword and tapped the squire lightly on the shoulders three times and made a short declaration such as 'In the name of God and Saint George, I make you a knight.'
Knights protected their lord's lands and fought in his battles against other lords. But knighthood was more than just fighting; it was also about chivalry. This meant
25 they had to be brave and honourable, to protect the honour of women and to protect the weak.

(based on: http://www.mnsu.edu/emuseum/history/middleages/knighthood.html)

Words
- *manners:* Benehmen
- *apprentice:* Lehrling
- *weapon:* Waffe
- *armour:* Rüstung
- *take confession:* beichten
- *bless:* segnen
- *kneel, knelt, knelt:* knien
- *chivalry:* Ritterlichkeit

Becoming a lady

Noble girls did not usually live with their parents. They lived in a monastery or another castle. There they were taught how to sew, to read and write and to sing. When they were fourteen, their parents chose a husband for them and they got married. On her wedding day, a girl wore her best clothes and with her husband
5   led a procession to the church door. The ceremony took place on the steps of the church. Then they had a huge party with food, wine and entertainment.

The husband was the head of the household in the Middle Ages and his wife was his property. A lady's main job was to care for the children. She was also responsible for the castle's kitchen and meals. She oversaw the cooks and servants, often kept accounts and made menus. When guests arrived at the castle, she had to entertain them.

Medieval ladies had expensive clothes that followed the latest fashion and they wore jewellery of gold or silver. They sprayed perfume around their rooms and their bodies to get rid of bad smells.

The ladies did many different things for fun. They did not go on boar hunts like men, but they liked hunting with trained falcons. They also liked to have picnics or play board games such as chess.

But ladies did not only do lady-like work. When their husbands were away in a battle, they were often responsible for the castle – and they usually did their job very well. In times of crisis, they even defended their castles against armies or they led armies on the battlefield.

Words

- *monastery:* Kloster
- *property:* Besitz
- *responsible for:* verantwortlich für
- *oversee, oversaw, overseen:* überwachen
- *keep accounts:* die Buchführung machen
- *get rid of:* etwas loswerden
- *boar hunt:* Wildschweinjagd
- *chess:* Schach

2 Choose the right answer and see how many you get right.

1 How old were the boys when they began their education as pages?
A ☐ 5 years old
B ☐ 7 years old
C ☐ 9 years old

2 What did a page not have to learn?
A ☐ to play the lute
B ☐ to sing
C ☐ to cook meals

3 What happened in the knighting ceremony?
A ☐ The lord tapped the knight on the head.
B ☐ The lord made a short declaration.
C ☐ The knight had to sing and dance before the ladies.

4 What did a girl not have to learn?
A ☐ to read Latin
B ☐ to sing
C ☐ to cook meals

5 How old were the girls when they got married?
A ☐ 14 years old
B ☐ 18 years old
C ☐ 24 years old

6 What did a lady have to do?
A ☐ cook meals for guests
B ☐ look after the castle when her husband was away
C ☐ go on boar hunts

Wenn ihr viele richtige Antworten hattet: Warum hat es so gut geklappt?

Wenn ihr wenige Punkte hattet: Warum hat es nicht so gut geklappt? Was könntet ihr beim nächsten Mal besser machen?

Going CLIL **49**

Scenario 6: Of knights and ladies

LAT Converting into language

A monk's life

1 Describe the daily life of a monk. Choose eight pictures and write one sentence for each picture.

#	Time	Activity
1.	midnight:	hold first service
2.	1 am:	back to bed
3.	6 am:	hold second service
4.	7 am:	breakfast in silence: bread & beer
5.	8 am:	work (e.g. copy books)
6.	9 am:	hold third service
7.	10 am:	daily meeting
8.	11 am:	hold High Mass
9.	12 am:	dinner: no meat
10.	2 pm:	hold fifth service
11.	3 pm:	work
12.	4 pm:	hold sixth service
13.	5 pm:	more work
14.	6 pm:	supper: bread & beer
15.	7.30:	go to bed

Example

At midnight the monks had their first service.

Du weißt sicher noch, welche Zeit man für Vergangenes verwendet?

2 Mönche führten ein hartes Leben. Was meinst du, warum sie Mönche wurden?

LAT Memorizing

Tournaments and banquets

1 Work together with a partner. Your teacher will tell you which text you should work on.
  a Read the text and make sure you understand it.
  b Say what the underlined words mean.

2 With your partner, decide who wants to be which person. Then learn your roles and perform the dialogue in front of the class.

At the tournament 1

Reporter:	Ladies and gentlemen, we are here at the tournament in Oakhampton. I'm speaking to Lord Edward. Lord Edward, in tournaments knights show how well they can fight. Can all knights just come and fight in the tournament?
Edward:	No, only knights with an invitation are allowed to fight.
Reporter:	Oh, I see. So the knights come here to prove themselves?
Edward:	Correct.
Reporter:	And what do all the lords and ladies do here?
Edward:	Well, lords look for good fighters and they <u>hire</u> them for their armies.
Reporter:	And what about the ladies?
Edward:	Ladies just like to watch the brave fighters and cheer for their favourite knights.

At the tournament 2

Reporter:	Hello, Sir John. You fought well today. Tell us something about the fight.
John:	I fought against Sir Andrew and I won!
Reporter:	Congratulations. How did you win?
John:	I pushed the other knight out of his <u>saddle</u> with my lance. Sometimes fighters get badly hurt or die – but Sir Andrew was all right.
Reporter:	Did you win a prize? What did you win?
John:	I won Sir Andrew's armour, his weapons and his horse.
Reporter:	Lucky you. My last question. You are one of the best fighters – do you have a talisman?
John:	Well, yes, I do. This morning I got Lady Ann's scarf and I showed it when I was fighting.

Words
- *fight, fought, fought:* kämpfen
- *prove yourself:* sich beweisen
- *brave:* tapfer
- *cheer:* jubeln
- *scarf:* Schal
- *weapon:* Waffe

Scenario 6: Of knights and ladies

Words
- *banquet:* Bankett, Festessen
- *it seems:* es scheint
- *bad example:* schlechtes Vorbild

Manners 1

Lady Caroline:	Guess what happened yesterday.
Lady Mary:	Oh please tell me!
Lady Caroline:	I was at the banquet at Castle Leoch.
Lady Mary:	Oh, let me guess – it's a story about Lord Robert.
Lady Caroline:	Yes, it is. He sat next to me and he talked to me with his mouth full!
Lady Mary:	Oh my goodness! A knight shouldn't do that! Is that really true?
Lady Caroline:	Of course it is. And when I looked at his hands I saw that they were dirty!
Lady Mary:	Oh no! That's horrible. I'm glad that I wasn't there to see it.

Manners 2

Teacher:	Well, page Harry, I saw you at the banquet yesterday. It seems that you have forgotten everything about <u>table manners</u>!
Harry:	Why? What did I do wrong?
Teacher:	Well, you had a cold. And you <u>blew your nose</u> with your hands!
Harry:	But Lord Robert does it too. And he knows his manners.
Teacher:	Lord Robert? You mean Lord Robert with the dirty hands?
Harry:	He is a fighter, a knight! Why should he wash his hands?
Teacher:	Well, maybe Lord Robert should come to my lessons too! He is a bad example for all pages.

Words
- *battle:* Schlacht
- *weapon:* Waffe
- *servant:* Diener

People 1

Reporter:	Hello, I'm a reporter from *Horse and Lance*. Can I ask you some questions?
Harry:	Yes, of course.
Reporter:	Aren't you Harry, Lord Michael's son?
Harry:	Yes, I am.
Reporter:	What are you doing here at this tournament?
Harry:	Well, I am page to Lord Robert. I help him get dressed in the morning and I bring him food and drinks.
Reporter:	Oh, you're a page. But you are only eight or nine years old!
Harry:	I'm eight. My father sent me to his friend Lord Robert when I was seven.
Reporter:	I see. What do you have to learn as a page?
Harry:	I have to learn to read and write, to sing and dance, to ride a horse, and of course good manners.

People 2

Reporter:	Hello, I'm a reporter from *Horse and Lance*. Can I ask you some questions?
William:	Well, yes.
Reporter:	You are a squire, is that right? How old were you when you became a squire?
William:	When I was 14 I became Lord Michael's squire, so I am his personal servant.
Reporter:	How do you help your master?
William:	I look after his horses, I <u>polish</u> the weapons and armour and I serve him at mealtimes.
Reporter:	And when your master goes to battle?
William:	I follow him and try to <u>protect</u> him.
Reporter:	And when are *you* going to be a knight?
William:	When I'm 21.

3 Listen and speak
   a   Record your dialogue.
   b   Enter the web-code GO310517–53 and listen to the dialogue. Did you get the pronunciation right?
   c   Record your dialogue once more until the pronunciation is correct.
   d   Act out your dialogue in front of the class.

4 Present and listen
Each group will present their dialogue. The others must listen carefully and answer the questions below.

At the tournament
1   Who fights at a tournament?
2   Why do lords watch tournaments?
3   Why do the ladies watch tournaments?
4   Was Sir Andrew injured?
5   What did Sir John win?
6   What was Sir John's talisman?

Manners
1   Where was Lady Caroline?
2   What did Lord Robert do?
3   What does Lady Mary think about this?
4   What did Harry do wrong at the banquet?
5   Harry thinks that Lord Robert does not need to wash his hands. Why?
6   What should Lord Robert do?

People
1   What job does Harry do?
2   When was Harry sent to Lord Robert?
3   What does he have to learn?
4   When did William become a squire?
5   What does a squire do?
6   What does William do when his master goes to battle?

Scenario 6: Of knights and ladies

Content and language workout

Rounding off

1) What did they do?
On the left, there is a list of medieval people, and on the right, a list of activities. Make sentences to show who did what in the Middle Ages.

> **Example**
>
> Knights went to tournaments.

Ladies

Squires

Pages

Knights

Monks

fight in battles
polish the lord's armour
learn to sew
learn good manners
hold services
play the lute
serve at meals
protect the honour of women
copy books
go on hunts with falcons
get up at midnight
cheer for a knight

Achte darauf, welche Zeit du hier verwenden musst!

___
___
___
___
___
___
___
___
___

2 **A motte-and-bailey today**
This is the picture of the motte-and-bailey in Pickering, North Yorkshire today.
A lot has changed since its construction in 1070.
Write six sentences to describe what has changed and what is still there.

Example

Three houses are still there.

The tower has disappeared.

Scenario 7: Paradise in danger

Getting started

We all live in the forest

Today, many rare animals carry small transmitters so that scientists know where they live and move.

1. Look at the list of animals below. They all live in the rainforest. What do the letters W, E, S, N stand for?

A	Capivara:	3° 08' 50" S	64° 58' 37" W
B	Orang-utan:	1° 46' 18" S	111° 30' 34" E
C	Bird of paradise:	5° 07' 12" S	139° 09' 07" E
D	Jaguar:	9° 41' 38" N	83° 37' 71" W
E	Mountain gorilla:	1° 25' 24" S	29° 32' 66" E

This is what you say: 'The Capivara is at a longitude of 3 degrees 8 minutes and 50 seconds south and a latitude of 64 degrees 58 minutes and 37 seconds west.'

2. Find the animals' signals and say which countries or regions they are from.

Do you remember the lines of longitude and latitude? Can you find the exact locations with the help of Google Earth?

56 Going CLIL

LAT Extracting meaning

Paradise under threat

1. What's hiding there?
   a Enter the web-code GO310517–57 and click on the link that appears. In the animation you can move between two areas of the rainforest: the

   _____ floor ('Krautschicht')

   and the _____ ('Hauptkronendach').

   b Find out what plants or animals live in the rainforest. Write down the names of five plants or animals and a sentence about each of them.

Plant/Animal	Information

2. Living in danger

   Find the orang-utan and click on it. The new window lists three dangers to the rainforest. Write down the words and explain in one sentence what they mean (in English or German).

Danger	Explanation

Going CLIL 57

Scenario 7: Paradise in danger

LAT Productive viewing

A closer look

1. Enter the web-code GO310517–58. Get together in groups and watch the video about the rainforest floor, the canopy or about deforestation. Don't worry if you don't understand every word – try to get the most important things.

Words
- *layer:* Schicht
- *the least:* am wenigsten
- *soil:* Erdboden, Humus
- *root:* Wurzel
- *gap:* Lücke

_____

Canopy

_____

_____

Rainforest floor

_____

The rainforest floor

The rainforest is like the different layers of the _____. The forest floor gets the least _____, so only _____ that don't need much light can grow there. There is only a thin layer of soil, so the roots of the _____ cannot go very deep. So many trees have _____ that keep them from falling over. When a tree falls over, it leaves a gap and sunlight can reach the _____. Streams and _____ are other places where the sunlight reaches the forest floor.

Words
- *species:* (biologische) Art
- *humidity:* Feuchtigkeit
- *root:* Wurzel
- *live off:* leben von
- *store:* speichern

The canopy

In Costa _____ there is now an aerial tram so people can watch the canopy. In the canopy there are _____ of species of trees. As you go _____, the climate changes. There are greater _____ of humidity and temperature and there is more _____. There are also some very special plants: Epiphytes don't have normal roots. They live off the _____ and _____. Bromeliads can store _____ in their leaves. Animals like _____ and _____ live in them. There are also _____ of different species of orchids.

Deforestation

Rainforests are cut at an alarming rate so that people can get wood and clear land for _____ and _____. In Brazil a _____ was built through the Amazon Region. From _____ to _____ over 5 million acres of forest land were cleared each year. Tribes living there have lost their homes and have nowhere to go. Much of the rainforest is being cut to create pastures for cattle. The soil is so _____ that you can grow things there for only a few years. Erosion 💡 is also a big problem: When there are no _____ to protect the earth's floor from the rain, the _____ washes away.

Words
- *at an alarming rate:* in bedrohlichem Tempo
- *clear:* räumen (hier: abholzen)
- *tribe:* (Volks-)Stamm
- *pasture:* Weide
- *cattle:* Vieh
- *soil:* Erdboden, Humus
- *protect:* schützen

❷ Fill in the blanks in the text about your topic.

❸ Here's something for the real experts. Take notes on your topic – in English or in German. Then write a script for your video and present it to the class while the video is playing without sound.

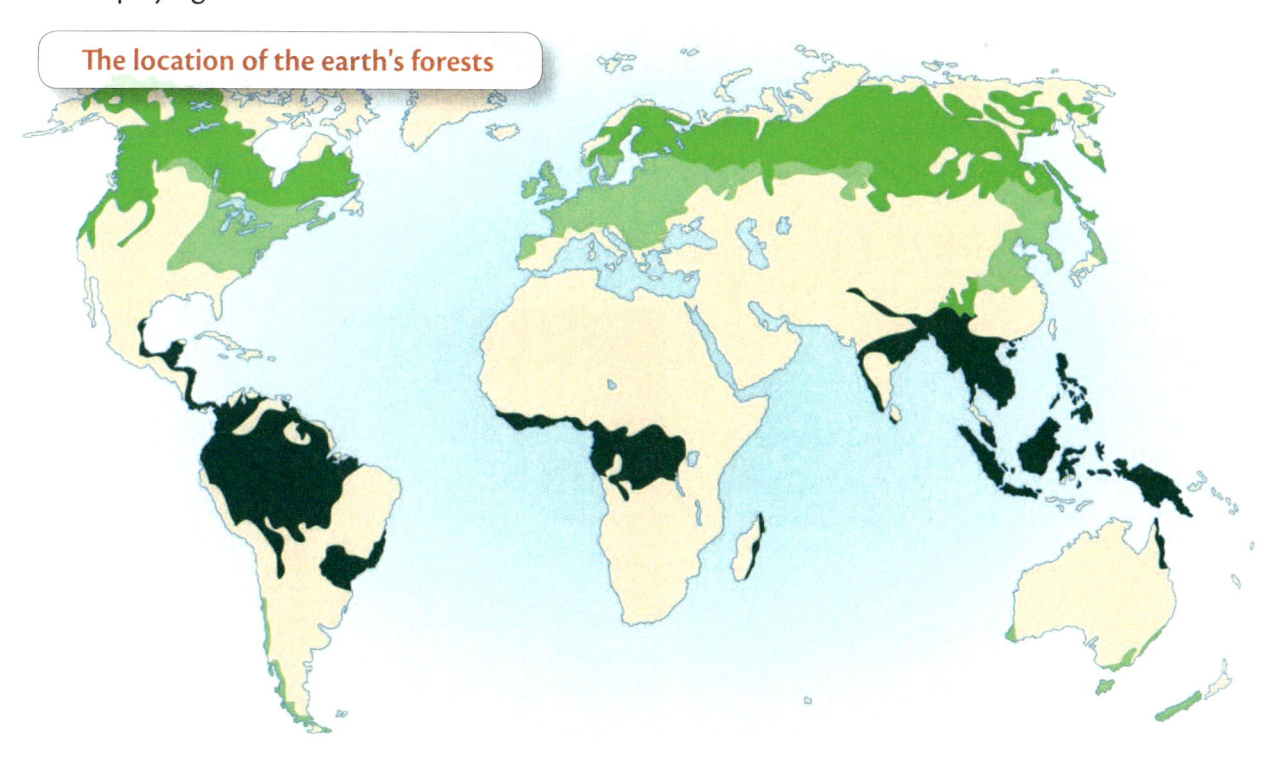

The location of the earth's forests

■ Tropical rainforests (tropische Regenwälder)
■ Boreal forests (boreale Regenwälder)
■ Temperate broadleaf and mixed forests (Laub- und Laubmischwälder)

Going CLIL **59**

Scenario 7: Paradise in danger

LAT — Converting into language

What happens if …

The following diagram tells you what happens when more and more tropical rainforests are cut down.

1 Write a text in English or in German to describe the consequences of deforestation. You may have a look at the animation again (web-code GO310517–58). Click on 'deforestation' and read the text about it.

Words
- *burn:* verbrennen
- *logger:* Holzfäller
- *habitat:* Lebensraum
- *survive:* überleben
- *emit:* ausstoßen
- *carbon dioxide:* Kohlendioxid

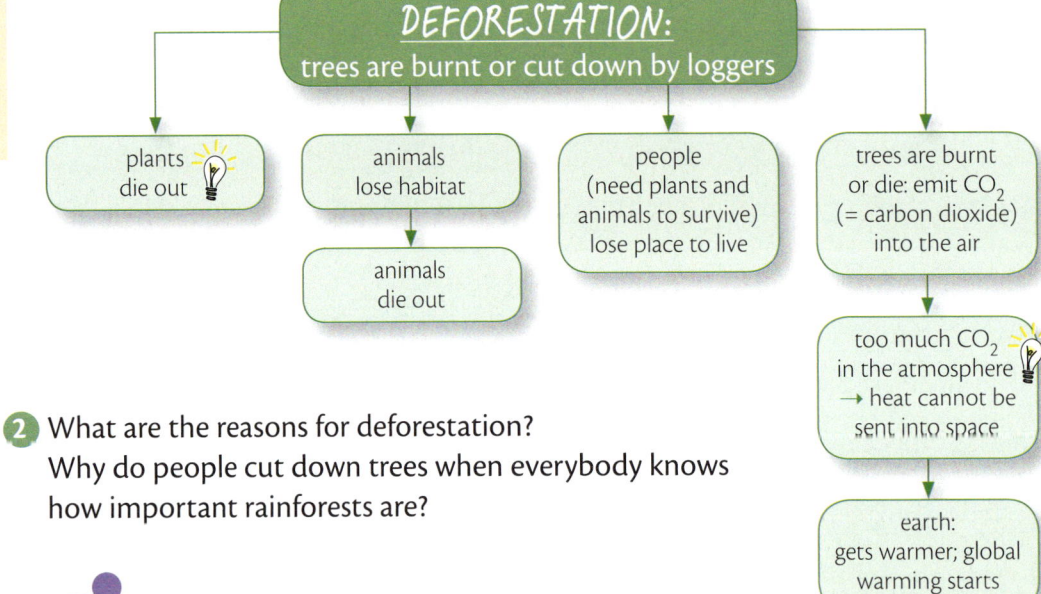

DEFORESTATION: trees are burnt or cut down by loggers

- plants die out
- animals lose habitat → animals die out
- people (need plants and animals to survive) lose place to live
- trees are burnt or die: emit CO_2 (= carbon dioxide) into the air → too much CO_2 in the atmosphere → heat cannot be sent into space → earth: gets warmer; global warming starts

2 What are the reasons for deforestation?
Why do people cut down trees when everybody knows how important rainforests are?

LAT — Working with pictures

The future of rainforests

What will rainforests look like in the future? Look at the pictures and write a short text with your ideas.

Du weißt sicher, welche Zeitform du hier verwenden solltest?

60 Going CLIL

LAT Memorizing

What do they mean to me?

Learn the poem by heart and perform it in front of the class.

Rain Forests

They're really half a world away,
There's nothing we can do.
'Rain forests' might be just two words
To kids like me and you.

They're really somewhere over there.
I may not even see
A rain forest in my entire life.
What should it mean to me?

I know that in these rain forests
That I may never see,
Half the world's plants, animals and insects
Live in harmony.

I know that trees are being cut,
Faster than we know.
These trees are where the creatures live,
So now where will they go?

So, I know they're half a world away,
Rain forests I can't see.
But I can learn and understand
Because the future starts with me!

Words
- *might be:* (hier) sind vielleicht
- *entire:* ganz
- *cut trees:* Bäume fällen

From: www.songs4teachers.com

Scenario 7: Paradise in danger

Content and language workout

Rounding off

1. In which layer do these animals and plants live? Tick ✔ in the table below.

Canopy layer

Rainforest floor

	Canopy layer	Forest floor
Bearded pig		
Epiphytes		
Flying fox bat		
Leopard cat		
Orang-utan		
Orchid		
Rafflesia		
Wallace's flying frog		

Orchid

Leopard cat

Epiphytes

Flying fox bat

Wallace's flying frog

Orang-utan

Rafflesia

Bearded pig

62 Going CLIL

2. Fill in the blanks.

Animals lose their _____ and may begin to _____.

Deforestation

_____ burn or _____ trees.

Dead trees give off _____ _____ into the atmosphere. This causes _____ _____.

_____ that depend on trees also begin to die out.

People who live in the rainforest also need the plants and the animals to _____.

Scenario 8: The hobbits of Flores

Getting started

Small creatures

You are going to listen to a report with the following words in it:

hobbit, little elephant, hunt, dragon, skeleton, island of Flores.

Imagine what the report could be about.

a Use the words to write a story in 5–6 sentences.

Words
- *hunt:* jagen
- *dragon:* Drache

_____

_____

_____

_____

_____

b Get together in groups of 3–4 and discuss which story you like best.

c Use the best ideas from your stories to write one story for your whole group.

d Choose one speaker to read your group's story to the class. In class, decide which story you like best.

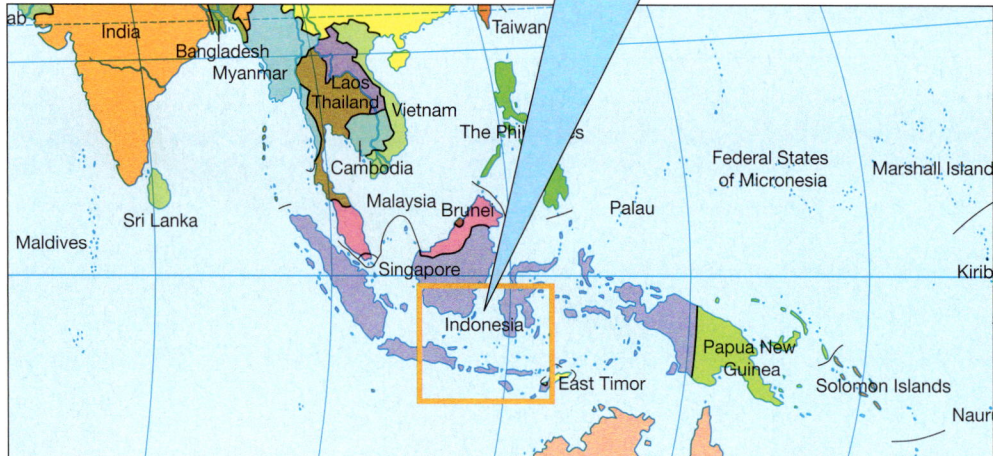

64 Going CLIL

LAT Productive listening

The little people of the forest

On the small island of Flores in Indonesia, scientists 💡 have made an interesting discovery.

a Get together in groups of three. Each pupil will get a letter (A, B or C) and a question.
b Listen to a report about the discovery and take notes on your question.
c Find others who have the same letter. Compare and check your notes with them.
d Report your findings back to your original group. Make notes on what the others tell you.

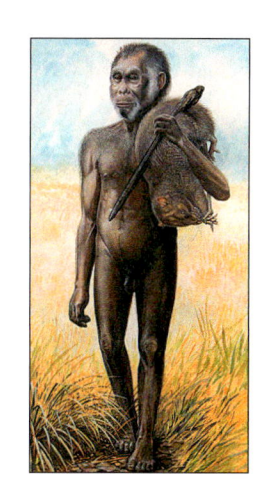

Questions

Group A: What discovery are the people talking about?

Group B: What stories were told about the people who lived on the island of Flores?

Group C: What did the experts 💡 find out about the body they discovered?

LAT Extracting meaning

One of us?

1) Your teacher will now divide the class into three groups. Each group gets a different text from the TV show, but the tasks are the same.

a Take notes on important facts.
b Compare your notes with other members of your group and agree on the most important points.
c Report your findings to the class.

Text A:

A new species?
Some experts believe that the Flores people are human beings; some think that they are a new species.

Words

- *human being*: menschliches Wesen
- *species*: (biologische) Art

Going CLIL **65**

Scenario 8: The hobbits of Flores

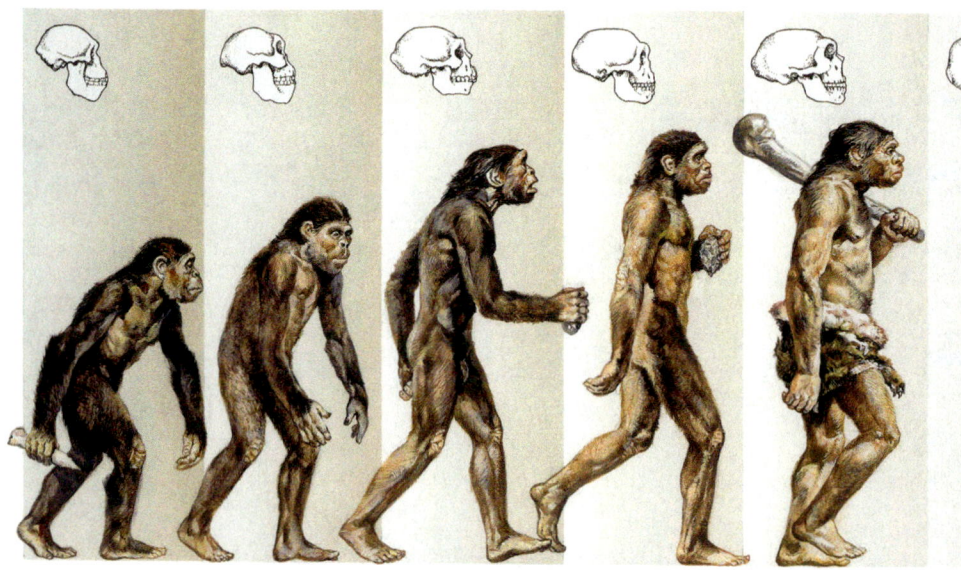

Words

- *disease*: Krankheit
- *brain*: Gehirn
- *skull*: Schädel
- *brain cavity*: Gehirnvolumen

The following notes may help you:
human:
- disease
- slow growth

new species:
- skulls different
- brain cavity

Text A: A new species?

Teuko Jacob: I think the woman we found is one of us. She's human, but she had a rare disease. That's why she has a small brain. The disease is called microencephaly.

Robert Krulwich: Microencephaly can make modern people grow more slowly. So she's one of us with a growth disease?

Teuko Jacob: I'm sure about it.

Richard Roberts: You're wrong. There's no chance at all that it's an individual of our species.

Robert Krulwich: So, since this debate is very complicated, I visited Ralph Holloway, one of the world's top skull experts and asked him, 'So, the woman was really small, wasn't she?'

Ralph Holloway: Yes, smaller than many chimpanzees.

Robert Krulwich: And since he's got a model of the lady's skull, I asked him, 'Does it look like our species? Like Homo sapiens? That is a human being. Do the new creatures that you've seen look like this?'

Ralph Holloway: No.

Robert Krulwich: No. Are they different in some way?

Ralph Holloway: Absolutely.

Robert Krulwich: Ralph has examined her brain cavity, and it's not like ours, he says.

Ralph Holloway: It's low. It's broad.

Robert Krulwich: You're sure of this?

Ralph Holloway: Absolutely.

(adapted from: www.pbs.org)

Text B:

Why they are so small

The experts explain how the Flores people got to the island and why they are so small.

Text B: Why they are so small

Robert Krulwich: So this might be a brand new sort of human. If that is true, how did this creature become so small?
The Australians believe that Homo floresiensis comes, as we do, from the original, earlier human, Homo erectus, who came out of Africa and went to Europe and Asia. But as experts can tell, the Homo erectus probably wasn't able to build boats. So how did they get to the island?
Jared believes that early humans reached Flores by a land bridge.

Jared Diamond: All this was going on during the Ice Ages, when, around the world, water was mostly found in the form of glaciers, so sea level was low.

Robert Krulwich: So what we know as water today was land back then. You could have walked there?

Jared Diamond: No, you couldn't walk there, but the water gaps were narrower.

Robert Krulwich: Those gaps were so narrow that it was easy to swim or float across. Other creatures did.

Jared Diamond: Elephants did it. Monkeys did it. If monkeys could do it, why couldn't these dumb humans do it? The reason is this: After they got there, the Ice Age ended. Glaciers melted, the ocean rose, and these early humans couldn't leave. And this may explain why they got so small.

Richard Roberts: They get small on an island where there are no major predators and where there is not that much food, so you really shouldn't eat any more than you need to if you want to survive. So for reasons of survival, it's more efficient to stay small.

Robert Krulwich: So you're not surprised then that this group of human-types could become very small?

Jared Diamond: There are lots of big animals that arrive on small islands, which then get smaller over time.

(adapted from: www.pbs.org)

Words

- *Ice Age*: Eiszeit
- *glacier*: Gletscher
- *sea level*: Meeresspiegel
- *gap*: Lücke
- *narrow*: schmal
- *melt*: schmelzen
- *predator*: Raubtier

The following notes may help you:
- land bridge
- Ice Age, glaciers, sea level
- narrow gaps
- glaciers melt, sea level
- no major predators, not much food
- people small

1.80m — Modern man
1.06m — Flores people

Scenario 8: The hobbits of Flores

Text C:

Small and smart
The experts explain how little people with little brains can do very smart things.

Words
- *a third*: ein Drittel
- *brain*: Gehirn
- *stone tool*: Steinwerkzeug
- *evidence*: Beweis
- *cave*: Höhle
- *campfire*: Lagerfeuer
- *might*: (hier) könnte(n)
- *sophisticated*: weit entwickelt
- *dwarf*: Zwerg
- *spit*: Spucke

Komodo dragon

Dieser Satz enthält viele Wörter, die du gar nicht kennen kannst, aber du kannst bestimmt das Wichtigste verstehen: Die Spucke war hochgiftig.

The following notes may help you:
- one third
- smart things
- evidence: stone tools, elephants, Komodo dragons
- hunt in groups
- language

Text C: Small and smart

Robert Krulwich:	The amazing thing, though, is that their brains were a third of the size of our brains.
Ralph Holloway:	Small, small. That's smaller than a chimpanzee's brain. But they used complicated stone tools that were difficult to make, didn't they?
Kerry Grant:	The evidence shows us that something with such a little brain may have been able to do more things than we originally thought.
Robert Krulwich:	The Australians say they found, at the cave site, evidence of campfire, so the little people may have been cooking with fire. They found stone tools nearby that might or might not belong to them but they look quite sophisticated. And remember, these people hunted and ate dwarf elephants, so ... And, the paleontologists say they did okay hunting and eating those animals.
Jared Diamond:	Warm-blooded animals get smaller on islands. Cold-blooded animals often get bigger on islands, to fill the place left by lions and tigers that could not get out there.
Robert Krulwich:	The evidence suggests that little people ate Komodo dragons. And how heavy are they?
Jared Diamond:	Up to 500 pounds. But it's worse than that.
Robert Krulwich:	Because back then, apparently, Komodo dragons were even bigger, and if you get near their mouths ...
Jared Diamond:	Their spit contains bacteria and anthrax and other things you wouldn't want to get infected by, really nasty bacteria.
Robert Krulwich:	So, if you were three feet tall, you should hunt these animals in groups. Would that need some kind of signaling or language or 'Watch out, Joe! Here comes the dragon'?
Ralph Holloway:	Yeah, I really do think that hunting in groups, etc. needs language.
Robert Krulwich:	Language, tools, technology, maybe the little people did all that, but if they did it with brains a third our size, those brains would be very different, extremely different from ours.
Ralph Holloway:	And that might be one of the great lessons of this ...
Robert Krulwich:	Oh, you're saying that maybe this brain is organized differently so it can do more in a little space?
Ralph Holloway:	Oh, it's definitely organized differently, and it may have done more in only a little bit of space, absolutely.

(adapted from: www.pbs.org)

2 Enter the web-code GO310517–68 and watch the TV show.

4 Make a picture story about the Flores people. Here are some ideas: how the people got to the island of Flores, how they hunted, how they fought Komodo dragons, etc.
  a Get together in groups and collect ideas for your picture story.
  b Choose different episodes 💡 and decide which of you is going to work on which episode.
  c Present your picture stories in class and decide which story you like best.

LAT Working with pictures

Caveman news

As you have found out, small heads don't mean low intelligence. Now find out about the development of human skulls.

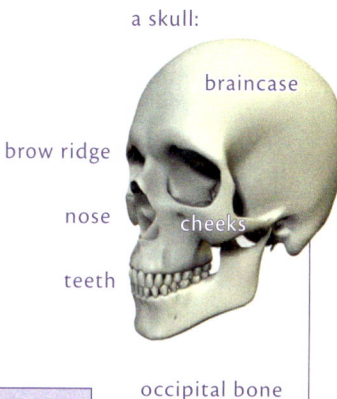

a skull:
braincase
brow ridge
nose
cheeks
teeth
occipital bone

1 Enter the web-code **GO310517–69** and click on the link that appears. Click on the two skulls.
  a Compare the skull of a Neanderthal to that of an early modern human, a Cro-Magnon. Fill in the table below.

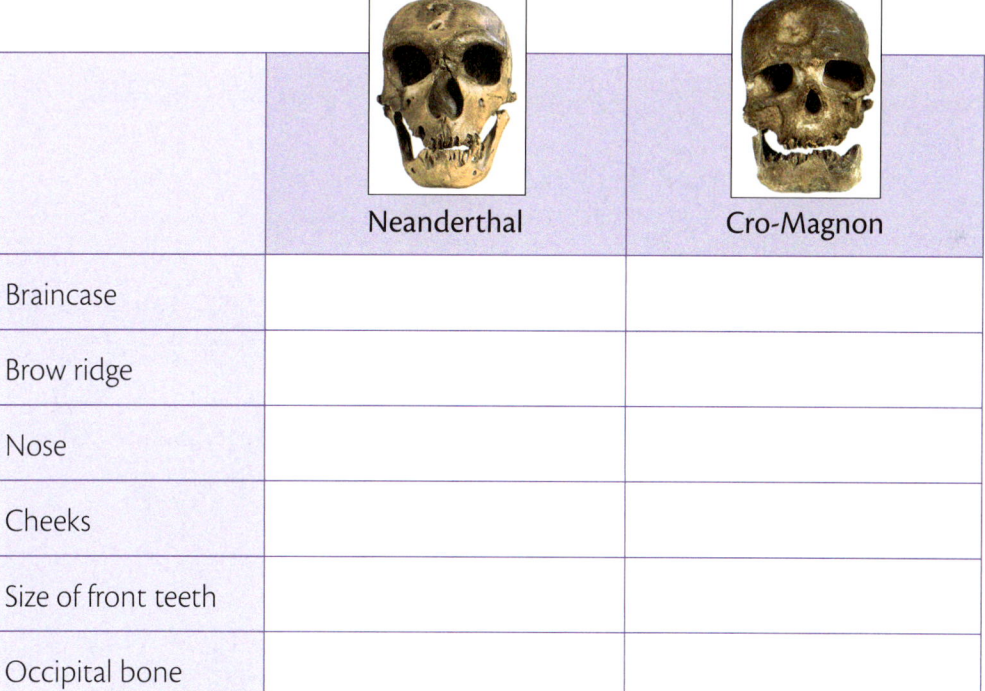

	Neanderthal	Cro-Magnon
Braincase		
Brow ridge		
Nose		
Cheeks		
Size of front teeth		
Occipital bone		

  b Describe the differences in 5–6 sentences.
  c Memorize the sentences.
  d Present your findings to the class.

Use adjective pairs like thick – thin, wide – narrow, big – small, etc.

2 Here's something for the real experts. Enter the web-code **GO310517–69** and watch the animation. Compare the brains of a chimpanzee to that of a modern woman and that of the Flores woman. You can use German if you like

Words
• *brain:* Gehirn

Scenario 8: The hobbits of Flores

3 Find out more about the development of man.

a Enter the web-code GO310517–70 and click on the link that appears. Do the 'Caveman challenge' and work on the following tasks.

Words
- *cave:* Höhle
- *man:* der Mensch
- *ape:* Affe
- *walk upright:* aufrecht gehen
- *body heat:* Körperwärme
- *hominid:* menschenähnliches Wesen

Stage 1: On two feet

Choose the correct ending of the sentence.

Apes started walking upright because …

- A ☐ … this saved energy.
- B ☐ … this made it easier to see and kill animals.
- C ☐ … this reduced body heat.
- D ☐ … this freed their hands to use tools.
- E ☐ … they could see further.

Stage 2: Food for thought

Tick ✓ the right answer. Which kind of food was better for early hominids?

- ☐ Meat
- ☐ Fruits and vegetables

Why? Ask your biology teacher for more information.

Stage 3: Tools

Match the tools on the left with their uses on the right.

Tools	Used for
scraper	antlers
harpoon	clothes
hand-axe	killing fish
hammerstone	choppers
spear thrower	animal carcasses
needle	animal hides
burin	throwing spears

70 Going CLIL

Stage 4: Firepower

Fill in the blanks.

Hominids started to use fire about _____ years ago. The first hominid that used fire was called _____. Cooked food was easier to _____, so our _____ could become _____.

Stage 5: On the hunt

Just play and relax!

Stage 6: Language

Fill in the blanks.
a Write down where you can find food.

Place	Food

b How long have humans been able to speak?

For at least _____ years.

Stage 7: Cave art

Fill in the blanks.

a Cave art is at least _____ years old.

b People painted caves because _____.

4 Enter the web-code GO310517–71 . Click on the links to find out more about stone age tools. Present the facts to your class.

Scenario 8: The hobbits of Flores

Content and language workout

Rounding off

1 Walking upright
Why did humans start to walk on two feet? Draw a picture for each reason.

2 Stone-age tools
Fill in the blanks and match the pictures with the sentences.

A Harpoons were used to _____.

B _____ were used to open animal carcasses.

C Needles were used to sew _____.

D Hammerstones were used to create _____.

3 Write a short paragraph about what hominids used to eat.

4 Create a poster about stone-age life.

Going CLIL **73**

Scenario 9: Snow in motion

Getting started

Snowy mountains

Interview your classmates and fill in the table.

a Write down at least two things that people like or don't like about skiing.

Find someone who …	Names	Ask him or her questions	Notes
… likes skiing.	_____ _____	'What do you like about it?'	_____ _____
… does not like skiing.	_____ _____	'What don't you like about it?'	_____ _____
… has had an exciting winter adventure.	_____ _____	'What happened?'	_____ _____

b Write 3–5 sentences about their winter adventure.

_____

_____

_____

_____

_____

- get lost
- break a leg / an arm
- no longer see your friends/family
- slip on the ice
- sleigh (drawn by horses/dogs)
- turn upside down
- fall down
- get dark
- overtake somebody narrowly
- hit your head
- get stuck in deep snow

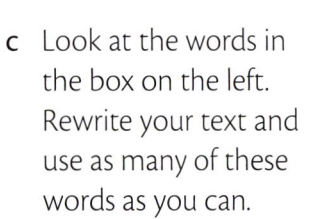

c Look at the words in the box on the left. Rewrite your text and use as many of these words as you can.

74 Going CLIL

LAT Productive listening

Caught in an avalanche

You are going to listen to a text about an avalanche. The following pictures will help you understand the text.

Words
- *avalanche:* Lawine

skier

guide

powder skiing

steep slope

flat slope

stability

ice crystals

conditions
"Die Konditionen waren ideal."

collapse

crack

cliché
Say the word out loud.

crevasse

cartwheel

somersault
flip over

equipment

helicopter

bruised

1 Read the questions, then listen to the text. Tick ✓ the correct answers. Sometimes there is more than one correct answer.

a Where do the people go skiing?
☐ Atlanta.
☐ Alaska.
☐ Alabama.

b How do the people get to the top of the mountain?
☐ They use a skilift 💡.
☐ They go up in a helicopter.
☐ They walk.

Going CLIL **75**

Scenario 9: Snow in motion

c What does the tour guide do before they start skiing?
- [ ] He makes a hole.
- [ ] He looks at some ice crystals.
- [ ] He jumps on the snow.

d The skiers go down the mountain …
- [ ] … together as a group.
- [ ] … one after the other.
- [ ] … together with the guide.

e How does the writer like the trip at first?
- [ ] He is scared.
- [ ] He feels alone.
- [ ] He likes it very much.

f What happens to his skis?
- [ ] They come off and go down the slope.
- [ ] They flip over.
- [ ] The writer loses one ski.

g What does the writer do to survive?
- [ ] He tries to stay on top of the snow and does cartwheels.
- [ ] He thinks about his family.
- [ ] He tries to stay as tall as possible.

h What does the writer do after the accident?
- [ ] He never goes skiing again.
- [ ] He goes on skiing for three days.
- [ ] He takes three days off.

2 Getting it right

a Work with your partner and put the sentences below in the right order.
b Compare your version to his or hers.
c Decide whose version makes the most sense.

A When the writer went down the hill, he really enjoyed it.
B The group arrived at the top of the slope that the guide had chosen for them. He looked a little bit worried.
C He made a hole to test the stability of the snow.
D Then he suddenly felt a movement behind him.
E On that day it was bright and sunny and it hadn't snowed for about three weeks.
F The writer went to Alaska with a group of friends who were all professional skiers.
G The guide went first.
H He saw that a crack was forming behind him.
I The guide was looking for an area where nobody had skied before.

Words
- *had chosen:* hatte ausgewählt
- *had snowed:* hatte geschneit
- *had skied:* war Ski gefahren

3 You are planning to go heli-skiing 💡 in Alaska next March.

Words
- *accommodation*: Unterbringung
- *availability*: Verfügbarkeit
- *offer*: Angebot

a Use the Internet to find out about prices, accommodation, availability, etc. Make notes.

Agency	Price	Accommodation	Availability	Extras

b Compare the different offers and decide in groups which one you like best. Report back to the class.
c Write an advert for your trip.

4 Discuss it
  a Do you think that heli-skiing should be forbidden 💡? Find out how many pupils in your class think so and present the results on a poster.
  b Get together in groups of four. Collect arguments for and against heli-skiing.

Reasons for heli-skiing	Reasons against heli-skiing
fun	expensive

c What is your conclusion? Make notes.
d Present your results to the class: Pupil number 1 gives an introduction, number 2 presents the reasons for heli-skiing, number 3 presents the reasons against it, number 4 presents the conclusion.

Words
- *conclusion*: Schlussfolgerung

Scenario 9: Snow in motion

LAT — Memorizing

A room with a view

For your heli-skiing trip you also need a hotel room.

a List the information you have to give and to ask for when you book a hotel room. Also think of problems that might come up.
b Compare your list with a partner.
c In pairs, write a short telephone dialogue between you and a hotel receptionist. Include one of the problems and find a solution.
d Memorize the dialogue and perform it.

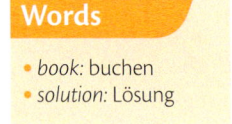

Words
- *book*: buchen
- *solution*: Lösung

LAT — Working with pictures

To the rescue!

1 The following pictures show a rescue mission after an avalanche.
   a Put the images in a meaningful order.
   b Write a headline for each picture.
   c Write a report about the rescue. Use your dictionary to look up words that you need.

Words
- *rescue*: Rettung

2 List the ten most useful words that you found and report back to the class.

3 Protect yourself and rescue others
   a Enter the web-code GO310517-78-1. Find out what you should do when you are in an avalanche and design a poster with instructions.
   b Enter the web-code GO310517-78-2. Find out which tools are used to rescue people and present your results to the class.

LAT Extracting meaning

The how and why of avalanches

1 Work in groups of three.
  a Each of you reads one of the texts below.
  b Try to guess the meaning of the underlined words. What helped you understand them?
  c Tell your partner about what you've just read.
  d Ask them to sum up what you've just told them to see if they've got it right.
  e Correct and help them if necessary. Swap roles.

Avalanches

When a huge mass of snow breaks away from the side of a mountain and moves down at great speed, we call this an avalanche. The danger of avalanches increases 1) in large snowstorms and 2) when the snow thaws.

In both cases, small things can trigger an avalanche: more snow, a skier, vibrations or even sound.

Avalanches only happen on slopes that are between 25 and 60 degrees steep. On steeper slopes, snow layers do not become thick enough, and on flat slopes, snow does not slide down easily. The rule of thumb is: A slope that is flat enough to hold snow but steep enough to ski on can cause an avalanche.

Words
- *thaw:* tauen
- *trigger:* auslösen
- *degree:* Grad
- *layer:* Schicht
- *slide down:* herunterrutschen
- *rule of thumb:* Faustregel
- *cause:* verursachen

Loose snow avalanches ('Lockerschneelawinen')

Loose snow avalanches normally happen in new or wet snow on a steep slope. They start at a point and become wider on their way down, so they have the form of a teardrop. There are two types. Loose snow avalanches that consist of wet, melting snow move slowly, less than 5 or 10 mph. Avalanches that consist of dry, powdery snow move very fast, usually at 75–100 mph, but sometimes they even go at 150 mph. Both types become as hard as a rock and are strong enough to destroy houses and forests.

Words
- *loose:* lose
- *teardrop:* Träne
- *consist of:* bestehen aus
- *melt:* schmelzen
- *mph:* miles per hour

Slab avalanches ('Schneebrettlawinen')

Slab avalanches happen when there is a strong layer of snow that breaks away and slides down the mountain. All the snow is set in motion at the same time. Sometimes it is only a thin layer of snow, but sometimes all the snow on a mountainside falls. There are hard and soft slabs. Soft slabs consist of fresh snow, and they can transform into hard slabs when they freeze. The slab is normally between 100–200 feet wide and travels at about 40 to 100 mph. 75 % of people killed in avalanches die in a slab avalanche.

Words
- *slab:* Platte
- *layer:* Schicht
- *slide down:* herunterrutschen
- *set in motion:* in Bewegung setzen
- *consist of:* bestehen aus
- *freeze:* gefrieren
- *wide:* breit

Scenario 9: Snow in motion

2 Fill in the numbers.

A Avalanches only happen on slopes that are between _____ and 60 degrees steep.

B Loose snow avalanches of wet, melting snow move at less than 5 or _____ mph.

C Avalanches that consist of dry, powdery snow usually move at 75–_____ mph, but sometimes they even go at _____ mph.

D The slab in a slab avalanche is usually between 100–_____ feet wide and travels at about _____–100 mph.

E _____ % of people killed in avalanches die in a slab avalanche.

3 Enter the web-code `GO310517–80` and click on the link that appears. Start the animation and describe what is happening.

4 The following pictures show you what people do to protect themselves from avalanches.

a Match the pictures to the words:

snow net
avalanche blasting
snow fence
avalanche shed
reforestation

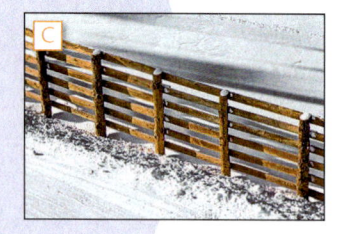

Words

- protect yourself: sich schützen

b Choose one picture and describe it.
c Read your description to the class and let the others guess which picture you are talking about.

LAT Converting into language

A good dog!

1 You are working for a newspaper in Canada. A friend has just told you about a rescue. Look at your notes, then write an article about what happened.

> First time – avalanche dog – save life – Canada
> Dog's name: Keno – find – skier Ryan Radchenko –
> get caught in avalanche
> Ryan: under snow – not able to free himself – mobile phone –
> call for help
> Small group – people – try find Ryan – but couldn't
> Keno – arrive at the accident – 10 minutes
> Start to sniff – run around – begin to dig – suddenly – bark loudly
> Keno – pull out – glove
> Others – start to dig – find – Ryan
> Ryan – alive – breathe – no big injuries
> Keno – get – reward – big steak

Words
- *get caught in:* erfasst werden von
- *sniff:* schnüffeln
- *dig:* graben
- *alive:* lebendig
- *breathe:* atmen
- *reward:* Belohnung

2 The next day you visit the place where Ryan was rescued. People are talking about what they were doing when the accident happened.

a Fill in the gaps.
b Try to find 1–3 more examples.

Use the verbs: go – land – play – race – sit

Example

"I was skiing near him when the snow caught him."

"I was _____ with Keno when the police called and told me that they needed Keno and me right away."

"We _____ in the office when the telephone rang."

"I _____ the helicopter when I my beeper went off."

"We _____ downhill when we saw Ryan fall down."

"I _____ away from the avalanche when it caught me."

Scenario 9: Snow in motion

Content and language workout

Rounding off

1 Fill in the gaps.

Avalanche:

When a mass of snow _____ at great speed, we call this an avalanche.

Slab avalanches …

… happen when there is a _____ of snow.

All the snow is _____ at the same time.

Loose avalanches …

… happen in _____ snow.

… have the form of a _____.

2 How do people protect themselves against avalanches?
List and describe four examples.

_____

_____

_____

_____

3 If you're caught inside an avalanche you should:

_____

Don't try to:

_____

If you want to rescue somebody from an avalanche, you can use:

_____

4 **Fill in the blanks to describe the pictures.**

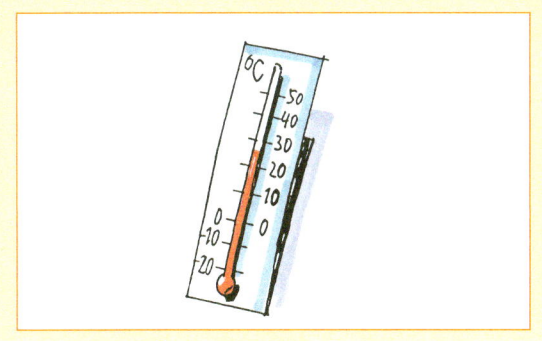

It's 25 _____.

The snowman is
_____.

Water is
_____.

a _____

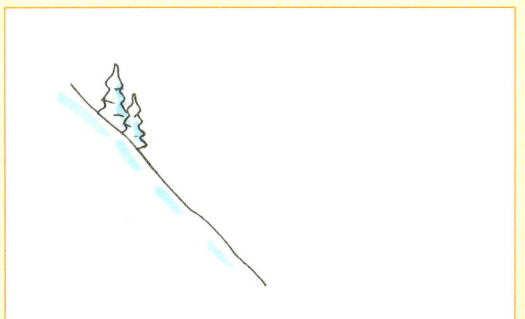

a _____

Skills pages

LAT ● Extracting meaning (Bedeutungen erschließen)

Wenn ihr englische Originaltexte, Filme o.ä. lest oder seht, gibt es dort häufig Wörter oder grammatische Formen, die ihr nicht kennt. Wir zeigen euch hier verschiedene Strategien, wie ihr damit umgehen könnt.

- ▶ Konzentriert euch auf das, was ihr versteht. Überlegt dann, worum es in dem Text gehen könnte.
- ▶ Nutzt dazu auch weitere Informationen, z. B. euer Hintergrundwissen oder Illustrationen, die den Text begleiten.

Wenn ihr wissen wollt, was ein einzelnes Wort bedeutet, können euch diese Strategien helfen:

- ▶ Überlegt, ob dieses Wort so ähnlich geschrieben oder ausgesprochen wird wie ein Wort aus dem Deutschen oder einer anderen Sprache, die ihr kennt.
  Z. B. *culture* → deutsch *Kultur* oder lateinisch *cultura*. Oder *chimpanzee* → deutsch *Schimpanse*.
- ▶ Seht genau hin, ob das Wort vielleicht ein Wort enthält, das ihr kennt.
  Z. B. *stormy* → *storm* oder *dancing lessons* → *dancing* + *lessons*.
- ▶ Manchmal hilft auch der Zusammenhang des Satzes: *We must hurry. Our train departs in three minutes*: *depart* → abfahren.

LAT ● Productive listening / viewing (aktives Zuhören / Filme sehen)

Das Verstehen ist oft schwierig, wenn Menschen sehr schnell sprechen oder Dialekte verwenden. So wird es trotzdem ganz einfach:

- ▶ Bevor ihr den Text hört, überlegt euch, worum es geht und was ihr über das Thema schon wisst.
- ▶ Lest die Aufgabe genau: Worauf sollt ihr überhaupt achten?
- ▶ Versucht nicht, jedes Wort zu verstehen. Achtet lieber auf den Gesamtzusammenhang.
- ▶ Lasst euch nicht verunsichern, wenn ihr einen ganzen Satz nicht versteht – hört einfach auf den nächsten Satz!
- ▶ Achtet auf Hintergrundgeräusche, z. B. Verkehrslärm oder eine Küchenmaschine. Dann wisst ihr schon mal, wo die Szene stattfindet.
- ▶ Versucht bei einem Film auch, aus den Bildern abzuleiten, worum es geht.

LAT ● Converting into language (Dinge versprachlichen)

Hier können euch ganz unterschiedliche Aufgaben begegnen, z. B. sollt ihr eine Karte oder Diagramme beschreiben oder Statistiken auswerten. Dabei werdet ihr oft das Gefühl haben, die nötigen Vokabeln nicht zu kennen. Versucht dann, mit den Wörtern auszukommen, die ihr kennt. Wenn euch ein bestimmtes Wort fehlt, versucht es anders auszudrücken:

- ▶ Nennt das Gegenteil: *the opposite of* → *It's the opposite of dark.* (*light*)
- ▶ Beschreibt die Sache: *It's an animal. It has dots. It lives in Africa, eats other animals and can run very fast.* (*a leopard*)
- ▶ Nennt einen Oberbegriff: *a kind of / a type of* → *It's a kind of fruit / It's a type of weather.*

LAT Describing pictures (Bilder beschreiben)

Wenn ihr Bilder beschreibt, solltet ihr genau sagen, was in welchem Teil des Bildes zu sehen ist.

Die folgende Skizze hilft euch dabei:

Wenn ihr schon mehr Erfahrungen mit Bildern habt, könnt ihr noch genauer werden:

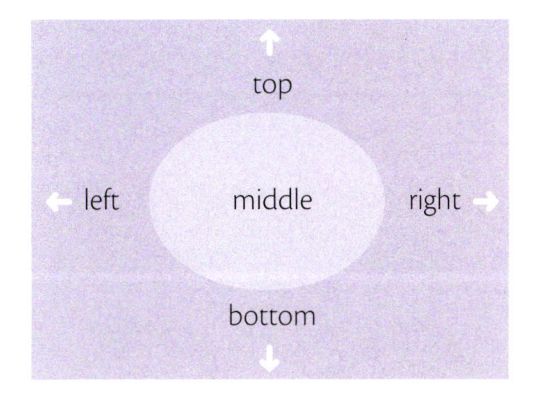

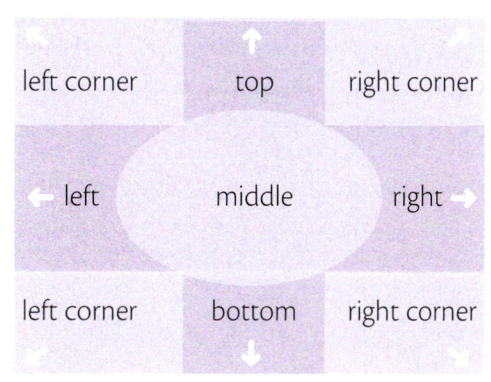

	↑	
← left	top middle	right →
	bottom ↓	

↖	↑	↗
left corner	top	right corner
← left	middle	right →
left corner	bottom	right corner
↙	↓	↘

Auch diese Wörter können euch helfen: *behind, between, in front of, next to, under*.

LAT Memorizing (Auswendiglernen)

Probiert einmal die verschiedenen Verfahren aus und wählt das aus, das ihr am besten beherrscht.

Satz für Satz wiederholen
▶ Lies den ganzen Text mehrmals genau durch.
▶ Lies den ersten Satz laut vor.
▶ Schließe die Augen und sprich den Satz aus dem Gedächtnis.
▶ Vergleiche ihn mit dem Original.
▶ Wenn du dich richtig erinnert hast, gehe weiter zum zweiten Satz. Wiederhole dann Satz 1 und 2 zusammen. Mach so weiter, bis du den ganzen Text kannst.
▶ Wenn du Satz 1 nicht korrekt wiedergeben konntest, wiederhole dieses Verfahren, bis du ihn kannst.

Auswischen / Abdecken
▶ Hierfür brauchst du eine Kopie oder einen Ausdruck des Textes.
▶ Lies den ganzen Text mehrmals genau durch.
▶ Decke ein paar Wörter mit Tipp-Ex ab und lies den Text mehrfach laut vor.
▶ Decke immer mehr Wörter ab, bis du schließlich den ganzen Text auswendig sagen kannst.

Karteikarten
▶ Lies den ganzen Text mehrmals genau durch.
▶ Schreib dir für jeden Satz ein oder mehrere Stichwörter auf Karteikarten. Sprich den Text laut vor.
▶ Streiche immer mehr Stichwörter so durch, dass du sie nicht mehr lesen kannst, und sage den Text laut.

Self-assessment pages

Damit ihr euren Lernfortschritt beobachten und festhalten könnt, könnt ihr auf diesen Seiten markieren ✏️, wie leicht oder schwer euch die jeweiligen Methoden fallen. Dann wisst ihr genau, woran ihr noch arbeiten müsst. Wenn ihr alle Zahnräder ausgemalt habt, seht euch an, wie sich eure Leistungen in den einzelnen Farben (=Methoden) verändert haben. Habt ihr euch verbessert?

Und so geht's:
Malt die Zahnräder aus, wie ihr euch einschätzt.

Daran muss ich noch arbeiten. (1 Ring)

Ich komme zurecht, brauche aber noch ein bisschen Übung. (2 Ringe)

Das ist überhaupt kein Problem. (3 Ringe)

Scenario 1 — From town to town

Getting to Nuremberg	Find your way through Limburg	What's where?	In town	Sightseeing
Memorizing	Productive listening/viewing	Working with pictures	Converting into language	Extracting meaning

Scenario 2 — Where I come from

Cornwall calling	Get active!	And where are you from?	Celina and Amy's home	Presenting Bavaria
Converting into language	Extracting meaning	Productive listening/viewing	Memorizing	Working with pictures

Scenario 3 — When in Rome …

Where are they?	On Marcus's heels	What happened?	Two dialogues	The gladiators
Working with pictures	Productive listening/viewing	Converting into language	Memorizing	Extracting meaning

Scenario 4 — Off to Europe

Images of Europe	Comparing Europe	Travelling to Europe	Paris crumpled up	A European exchange
Working with pictures	Productive listening/viewing	Converting into language	Extracting meaning	Memorizing

Scenario 5 — Stormy weather ahead

And now, the weather forecast for tomorrow	Weather by numbers	Rain in may	Palm trees in Ireland?	Weird weather
Memorizing	Converting into language	Working with pictures	Productive listening/viewing	Extracting meaning

Scenario 6 — Of knights and ladies

My home is my castle	Growing up in medieval times	A monk's life	Tournaments and banquets	
Working with pictures	Extracting meaning	Converting into language	Memorizing	

Scenario 7 — Paradise in danger

Paradise under threat	A closer look	What happens if …	The future of rainforests	What do they mean to me?
Extracting meaning	Productive listening/viewing	Converting into language	Working with pictures	Memorizing

Scenario 8 — The hobbits of Flores

The little people of the forest	One of us?	Caveman news		
Productive listening/viewing	Extracting meaning	Working with pictures		

Scenario 9 — Snow in motion

Caught in an avalanche	A room with a view	To the rescue!	The how and why of avalanches	A good dog!
Productive listening/viewing	Memorizing	Working with pictures	Extracting meaning	Converting into language

Quellenverzeichnis

Illustrationen

Roland Beier, Berlin (S. 37; S. 41 alle Illustrationen; S. 43 (A,B,C,D); S. 45 alle Illustrationen; S. 46 (A,B,C,D); S. 47 u.; S. 48–51 alle Illustrationen; S. 53; S. 70 u. (Tabelle); S. 73 (A,B,C,D); S. 75 (steep slope); S. 75 (flat slope); S. 75 (cartwheel); S. 75 (Somersault flip over); S. 75 (bruised); S. 81 alle Illustrationen u.; S. 83 alle Illustrationen); Dr. Volkhard Binder, Berlin (S. 5 o. r.; S. 6 o.; S. 10; S. 13 M.; S. 17 M.); Carlos Borell (S. 16)

Bildquellen

akg-images, Berlin (S. 71 M., S. 20 o. l.); Alamy, Abingdon (S. 4 o.: John Elk III; S. 4 M.: David Noble Photography; S. 4 r.; S. 12 u. l. u.: Sylvia Cordaiy Photo Library Ltd; S. 25: Lebrecht Music and Arts Photo Library; S. 26 o. l.: Content Mine International, S. 26 o. r.: The Print Collector; S. 26 u. r.: North Wind Picture Archives; S. 30 o. l.: Brian Hickey Photography; S. 30 M. r.: Marion Kaplan; S. 39 o.: Alex Segre; S. 40 M. l.: Ros Drinkwater; S. 40 M. r.: Nordicphotos; S. 44 M. l.: K-PHOTOS; S. 56 (B): Redmond Durrell; S. 56 (D): Edward Parker; S. 62 (8): Arco Images GmbH; S. 75 (12): Steve Bloom Images; S. 78 (E): SHOUT; S. 78 (G): blickwinkel; S. 80 (B): Worldwide Picture Library; S. 80 (E): TMI; The Art Archive, London (S. 70 u. l.: Gianni Dagli Orti; S. 73 M.: Gianni Dagli Orti; AP Associated Press, Frankfurt/M. (S. 2 (8); S. 65 u.); Avalanche.org (S. 78 (B); S. 79 u.); Bildarchiv Preußischer Kulturbesitz, Berlin (S. 23 u. l. Ausschnitt; S. 23 o. r. Ausschnitt; S. 23 u. r. Ausschnitt); Cinetext, Frankfurt/M. (S. 42 o. l. Standfoto The Day After Tomorrow, 2004); Corbis, Düsseldorf (S. 2 (5): Warren Faidley; S. 30 u. r.: Brendan Regan; S. 32 l.: Jan Butchofsky-Houser; S. 32 u. l.: Alinari Archives; S. 32 u. M.: Free Agents Limited; S. 42 o. r.: Eric Nguyen; S. 42 u. r.: Warren Faidley; S. 44 o. l.: Heide Benser; S. 44 u. l.: Jutta Klee; S. 55: Skyscan; S. 56 (C): Jack Fields; S. 57: Frans Lanting; S. 60 l.: Frans Lemmens/zefa; S. 60 u. M.: Envision; S. 61 o. r.: Kazuyoshi Nomachi; S. 61 M. (2): Frans Lanting, S. 61 M. (4): Kazuyoshi Nomachi; S. 61 u.: Frans Lanting; S. 62 r. (1): Wolfgang Kaehler; S. 62 r. (2): Winfried Wisniewski/zefa; S. 65 o. r.: Peter Shouten; S. 76: Lee Cohen, S. 78 (C): Christophe Boisvieux; S. 78 (D): Josef Mallaun/zefa; S. 79 M.: Galen Rowell; S. 81 o. r.: Hans Reinhard/zefa; S. 82 u.: F. C. Koziol); dkimages.com, London (S. 27 o. M.: John James / © Dorling Kindersley; S. 47 o.: Joanna Cameron / © Dorling Kindersley); Getty Images, München (S. 2 (4): Fred Tanneau; S. 30 o. r.: Fred Tanneau); Mareike Hölter, Berlin (S. 29 alle Bilder); karenswhimsy.com (S. 54 o. l. Sir Thomas Vaughn, published in: The Pictorial Edition of the Works of Shakespeare – Histories, Vol. II, ed. by Charles Knight, New York, ca. 1888); dieKLEINERT.de, München (S. 70 o. l.: Enno Kleinert); Mary Evans Picture Library, London (S. 2 (6) Ausschnitt; S. 54 u. l.; S. 54 M.; S. 71 u.); Mauritius Bildagentur, Frankfurt/M. (S. 2 (3); S. 20 u.; S. 80 (D)); Panometer GmbH, Berlin (S. 21 + 22 Ausschnitte: © Asisi, Ansicht des „Forum Romanum" von Yagedar Asisi für die Geo-Epoche-Publikation „Das römische Reich", 2001); Photolibrary, London (S. 12 o. l.: M & C Denis-Huot; S. 68: James Watt); Photo Researchers, Inc., New York (S. 26 M.: Georg Gerster); Picture Alliance, Frankfurt/M. (S. 2 (7): Stephen Dalton / NHPA / Photoshot; S. 20 M. r.: maxppp; S. 23 M. l.: Bildagentur Huber / G. Simeone; S. 27 o. l.: dpa-Film; S. 30 M. l.: ASA-Actionplus; S. 59; S. 62 r. (3): Okapia KG, Germany; S. 62 r. (4): Okapia KG, Germany; S. 62 r. (5): Stephen Dalton / NHPA / Photoshot; S. 62 (6); S. 62 (7): Okapia KG, Germany; S. 66 o.: De Agostini / World Illustrated / Photoshot / dpa; S. 70 Ausschnitt: De Agostini / World Illustrated / Photoshot / dpa; S. 72 o.: Johann Brandstetter / Okapia; S. 72 u.: Johann Brandstetter / Okapia; S. 78 (A): dpa / Fotoreport / epa / Keystone / Fabrice Coffrini; S. 78 (F): dpa / Fotoreport / Petter Kneffel; S. 78 (H): dpa / Report / Guillaume Bonnaud); Römisch-Germanisches Zentralmuseum, Mainz (S. 24); Shutterstock, Inc., New York/NY (S. 2 (2): Andrey Gatash; S. 2 (9): Steve Rosset; S. 4 u.: Sascha Burkard; S. 11 o. r.: Holger Mette; S. 11 u. r.: Kamil Sobócki; S. 12 u. r. o.: Jörg Jahn; S. 13 u. M.: Gail Johnson; S. 13 o. l.: Elisa Locci; S. 13 u. l.: Stephen Aaron Rees; S. 13 o. M.: Rachelle Burnside; S. 13 o. r.: Vasiliy Ganzha; S. 13 M. o. r.: Eline Spek; S. 13 M. u. r.: Joe Gough; S. 13 u. r.: Geir Olav Lyngfjell; S. 15 M. r.: Jaimie Duplass; S. 15 u. l.: Avner Richard; S. 17 r.: Andrey Gatash; S. 17 u. l.: MaxFX; S. 18 (Compass); S. 32 o. r.: pandadaw; S. 32 M. l.: Elena Elisseeva; S. 32 u. r.: jordi espel; S. 33 l.: Yuri Arcurs; S. 33 r.: Galina Barskaya; S. 38 (1): Gillian Mowbray; S. 38 (2): 6015714281; S. 38 (3): Joy Brown; S. 38 (4): photogl; S. 40 o. l.: Nik Niklz; S. 40 o. r.: Seleznev Oleg; S. 56 (A): dundamin; S 56 (E): Miranda van der Kroft; S. 40 M.: Zlatko Guzmic; S. 60 o.: Snowleopard1; S. 60 r.: Eric Gevaert; S. 66 u.: Kitch Bain; S. 74 o. l.: Galina Barskaya; S. 74 u. r.: Mag. Alban Egger; S. 75 (skier): Avner Richard; S. 75 (guide): Roca; S. 75 (powder skiing): Steve Rosset; S. 75 (crack): Armin Rose; S. 75 (Skier und Stöcke): Vallentin Vassileff; S. 75 (Skischuh): Blaz Kure; S. 75 (Handschuhe): viZualStudio; S. 75 (Helm): Vadim Ponomarenko; S. 75 (Brille): Jurijs Korjakins; S. 77 o.: Roca; S. 77 u.: Sergey Dubrovskiy; S. 78 o. r.: Steve Weaver; S. 79 o.: Steve Rosset; S. 80 (C): Milat); ullstein bild, Berlin (S. 2 (1): Imagebroker.net; S. 6 u.: Momentphoto; S. 8: Imagebroker.net; S. 15 u. r.: Imagebroker.net; S. 12 u. re u.: Wodicka; S. 12 u. M.: Imagebroker.net; S. 40 u.: Imagebroker.net; S. 61 o. l.:DIAGENTUR; S. 61 M. (1): AP; S. 61 M. (3): Still Pictures; S. 62 l.: Dohne; S. 63: Reuters; S. 69 l.: Granger Collection; S. 69 M.: Granger Collection, S. 69 r.: Imagebroker.net); Westdeutscher Rundfunk, Köln (S. 9 beide Bilder: Domke)

Titelbild

Shutterstock, Inc., New York (l.:Soundsnaps, r.:Tom Olivera)

Textquellen

S. 4: "A Small Town", text and music: John Cougar Mellencamp, 1985 by Full Keel Music Corp., für D/A/CH ehem. Ostblock ex. Baltic-Staaten: EMI Music Publishing Germany GmbH, Hamburg;
S. 31, 33: Tables: Tourism Statistics 1995–2006, based on the statistics published in: UNWTO World Tourism Barometer, published and printed by the World Tourism Organization, Madrid, 2007. http://www.unwto.org/facts/eng/pdf/barometer/unwto_barom07_2_en.pdf, © UNWTO, 9284401908;
S. 42–43: "Weird weather", abridged from the BBC broadcasting: Inside Out – South, 7 October 2002, http://www.bbc.co.uk/insideout/south/series1/weird-weather.shtml, © British Broadcasting Corporation, London, 2002;
S. 61: "Rain Forests", poem by © Mary Flynn, www.songs4teachers.com, Barrie/Ontario, Canada;
S. 66–68: "Text A: A new species?", "Text B: Why they are so small", "Text C: Small and smart", adapted from the science documentary: NOVA ScienceNOW, Public Broadcasting Service (PBS), airdate: 19 April 2005, http://www.pbs.org/wgbh/nova/transcripts/3209_sciencen.html#h01. From WGBH Educational Foundation, © 2005 WGBH/Boston

u. = unten; o. = oben; r. = rechts; l. = links; M. = Mitte